AN ELEPHANT IN THE LIVING ROOM

Is It Too Late To "Kill All The Lawyers"?

Wendell Whitney Thorne

authorHOUSE®

AuthorHouse™
1663 Liberty Drive, Suite 200
Bloomington, IN 47403
www.authorhouse.com
Phone: 1-800-839-8640

First published by AuthorHouse 4/27/2009

ISBN: 978-1-4389-6383-9 (e)
ISBN: 978-1-4389-6381-5 (sc)
ISBN: 978-1-4389-6382-2 (hc)

Library of Congress Control Number: 2009902975

Printed in the United States of America
Bloomington, Indiana

This book is printed on acid-free paper.

For Alexa, Caroline, Lennon & Cooper

"The first thing we do is kill all the lawyers."

William Shakespeare
Henry VI, Part II

Balance the cost of the Soul you lost
With the dreams you've lightly sold;
Are you under The Power of Gold?

Dan Fogelberg, "The Power of Gold"

TABLE OF CONTENTS

Introduction   ix

Foreword   xiii

A Lifetime of The Law   1

Who Are These Lawyers?   7

Rule No. 1. Never Take A Stand   29

31 Flavors of Law   43

Waffling Away Accountability   53

Felix Frankfurter's Crazy Invention   72

The Right To Life   91

Classical Mechanics and The Law   106

"Leveling The Playing Field"   118

Masticating The First Amendment   137

Defending The "Guilty"   159

Manufacturers' Never-Ending Liability   171

The Second Amendment:
  The People's Last Defense   186

Who's To Blame?   194

INTRODUCTION

Who could argue that the automobile is just about the one invention that most people in the United States simply cannot live without? Sure, in your larger cities the mass transit system is really handy and lots of people use subways and buses to get around. But once you get a bit out of these few metropolitan areas, you just about cannot live without your car.

Now, go to your telephone book, the yellow one. Take a survey of every business that has anything remotely to do with automobiles, including dealers, repair shops, painters, stereo installers, mufflers, tires, whatever. Use your imagination. Now, add up the pages.

Next, do the same thing with attorneys.

Amazing, isn't it? If your city or town is anything like mine, the number of pages dedicated to lawyers will significantly outnumber the ones having anything at all to do with automobiles, which, we all agree, are just about impossible to do without. This astonishing realization should scare you, but that's just the beginning of the story. [1]

The exponential bloom of attorneys—and the accompanying law they are sworn to uphold—in the United States in the last 35 years has made life, liberty and the pursuit of happiness darn near impossible. Laughable, in fact. Now that lawyers and their

---

1. According to the American Bar Association, there were 1,143,358 lawyers in the United States at the end of 2007. Add to that an average of 4 staff members for each lawyer, legislative staffs, professional expert witnesses, consultants and the like, and you can see how deeply this thing called "The Law" impacts our daily lives.

Law have decimated common sense and isolated money as the sole reason for living, the joke is on them. Literally. There are entire books devoted to nothing more than lawyer jokes. And, if they weren't so true, a lot of them would be pretty funny.

Most lawyers really take offense to jokes about lawyers. Some have even twisted Shakespeare's joke (*quoted in the subtitle and front pages of this book*), saying Dick the Butcher meant "let's *not* kill all the lawyers."

But, can you blame them? What, after all, do lawyers have to do with the endless sea of self-procreating law that permeates every fiber of our being throughout our entire life? I mean, can't we separate "The Law" from "The Lawyers"? The short answer, regardless of what the organized bar will tell you, is "no."

I'm a barber. Have been for a few years. I know what you're thinking: *What's a barber know about the law?* After all, wasn't it Tony Shaloub, portraying a lawyer in *The Man Who Wasn't There* who uttered the words, "I'm an attorney, you're a barber; you don't know anything."?

Truth is I used to be a lawyer. There were parts of it, lots of parts of it, actually, I really enjoyed. But there were parts of it, perhaps the most important ones, that I really never had the stomach for. I seriously thought about walking away from it after the first year of law school, but was convinced by a classmate—to whom I just happened to be married—to stick it out. So, I did, and I gave it a few of my best years. This book is a little bit about those years, but really more about the years that followed, even up to now.

And, despite what you may think, the critical issues that face each of us in life are often neatly ironed out inside the confines of the local barbershop. You wouldn't imagine the clarity and common sense that is uttered in the shop. Barbers and customers alike share in the give and take in this marketplace of ideas, often winnowing out the touchy-feely chaff that mucks up the pronouncements of politicians, educators, the media, sports and other celebrities and, of course, lawyers. What emerges from that process makes sense. What emerges from that process are solutions that work, if only somebody in charge of making those decisions would ask.

But nobody ever does.

Me? I'm the moderator. I'm the guy with the legal background who listens to it all, offering guidance when the discussion gets too far away from established legal tenets, and then smiles. It's fun. Sometimes I toss a ball in the middle of it and just watch to see how it all plays out. (*Okay, truth is that I'm the CEO of my tiny corner of the business world, and I get to say anything I want inside the confines of that corner without any potential repercussions from a boss or supervisor, and I often do so*). In a world hell-bent on a high-speed exodus from common sense truth and justice, these discussions keep me grounded, restore my faith in human nature, and give me hope for the future.

So everyday I balance in my mind what I know about the law and what I'm learning about people and I've come to the conclusion that there are things I believe in, in the grand scheme of life on Earth, that the Law does not and can not embrace because they are simple things. The Law is not a simple thing.

So this is one former lawyer's derivations of life in the United States under the thumb of a legal system that day after day ignores the will of the people and their common sense. And it is a message of hope for those who feel hopeless, helpless and resigned to an unsatisfying life in a country so careless with the truth.

A note regarding timing. I started writing this book several years ago, so some of the information is a bit dated and I've tried to footnote where I think it's necessary to do so. As a guy raising a family and running a pretty busy business, I don't have much time to write, so things have taken longer than I would have hoped. Thanks for understanding.

FOREWORD

It is New Year's Day, 2000. To my knowledge, neither the national electric matrix nor the worldwide computer network took a hit such as that predicted by the Y2K voices calling in the night. No television network or radio station shut down, nor did any aircraft or train or seagoing vessel go out of control and crash killing thousands. Or one. ATM's provided the appropriate services, and yielded correct balances. Heck, even our coffee maker came on as scheduled, at 6:50 A.M. My brother's eggs-in-one-basket hope for a new life, free from credit problems and court records, fizzled with the last dying sparkler.

The world goes on.

But this is the first year in a long time that opens its eyes to find me no longer practicing the law I had once loved; the law I had once believed needed my fresh, clear voice. The law that I felt I was born to practice.

For I have come to the awful conclusion that the law and her lawyers are uniquely responsible for much that is wrong in our world. People who live and work and pay and die can look to no other single place in modern society that so thoroughly dominates their thoughts and actions. The media makes sure we hear about the damages:

A foolish old man in Wisconsin chooses to ignore the warnings on his push-type lawn mower, and tilts it to one side to rinse the grass clippings from the blade—*while it is still running*—and pays for his mistake with most of the fingers on his left hand. The resulting lawsuit–one that no reasonable human being would even think of bringing–finds the manufacturer responsible for not having a device to automatically kill the engine whenever it is tipped at such an angle, and it has to pay for the man's fingers. It is a good thing the man was not a concert pianist or a professional fly-tier, or the price tag would have been much higher indeed...

An elderly woman (*I call her that because she is old, and I happen to believe that the "political correctness" of the term "senior citizen" is yet another casualty in a world in which lawyers have shaped the euphemistic jargon of our everyday speech in order to soften the natural blows inflicted by the truth of life itself*) who, like every other driver in the world, innocently and habitually places the hot container of coffee given her at the drive-up window at McDonald's between her legs. I do it. You do it. Once we take control of our beverages, they are *ours*. If they spill, it's *our* fault! Oh, I suppose it might be the fault of the coffee's container manufacturer, if it made a cup that couldn't withstand the heat; after all, McDonald's coffee *is* HOT (it says so right on the container!). It might even be our auto manufacturer's fault if some manufacturer defect caused it to lurch without warning. But there is no way, in the furthest stretch of a rational mind, that it is McDonald's fault. Yet, unless you've been under a rock, you know that a jury decided it was indeed McDonald's fault, and that to the tune of *over $4 million*. A judge overturned or "remittitured" the award to just over one million, but still, Americans get the message: Search for a way to make hay out of your own mistakes. It is America's latest pension plan and you needn't search very far.

I have watched as these cases, and countless others which have gone essentially unpublicized, defied logic, challenged morals and soured the palates of a society not so old as to have forgotten fairness, honesty, and common decency. For me, however, it was one case in particular that was to provide the greatest instigation, the last straw, for my exodus from the legal profession.

To an entire generation of avid football watchers, long before the remote control or the instant replay or television time outs or Gatorade, Orenthal Julius Simpson represented America. Coming from a less-than modest background, Simpson used his athletic prowess on the gridiron to become an All-American running back, first at the University of Southern California, and then in the NFL, where he labored with perennial losers, the Buffalo Bills, setting rushing records that would stand for decades.

Simpson utilized his star status to catapult him to a moderately successful film and television commercial career, all the while hiding from the camera a terrible secret. A secret that emerged only after his ex-wife and her friend were discovered brutally murdered outside her home in a Los Angeles suburb. As it turns out, Simpson was a jealous, controlling, violent man who, like many little boys living in adult male bodies, was unable to handle the stresses of life as a man—or to deal with rarely-encountered disappointment—and took out his aggression on his wife, one hate-filled blow at a time.

Losing control of his emotions, Simpson allowed them to overcome any sense of reason he may have had, and ultimately slaughtered his ex-wife, Nicole Brown, and her friend, Ron Goldman. You know it. I know it. Everybody knows it. Only a legal system exhibiting the same lack of control as Simpson's could ever have found the path to acquittal engineered by the likes of F. Lee Bailey, David Shapiro, and Johnny Cochran, three men I would not allow to enter my house for any reason.

Simpson walks the earth a free man[2], as free as his own soul will allow, anyway. Yes, a civil jury, not fettered with the stringent burden of proof of "guilt beyond a reasonable doubt" found in the criminal system, rendered Simpson legally responsible for Nicole's murder, and awarded the bulk of Simpson's personal wealth to Nicole and Ron's estates. But to the hundreds of millions of slack-jawed onlookers, that watered-down, mealy-mouthed result will never be enough to convince them that the law is not a product of the mind of Lewis Carroll, and that the Mad Hatter's Tea Party awaits all who enter the hallowed halls of "justice."

Anyway, it was enough for me. I decided I could never look another person in the eye if I chose to remain an active member of the bar. I decided that the law had done its level best to kick the humanity out of me, and I had persevered. The "class clown" of my law school, I realized I just wasn't able to seriously accept myself as perpetuator of the everyday miscarriages of justice, or to acquiesce in the triteness of the old "well, it's not perfect, but it's the best system in the world" parry.

I decided that I was no longer able to look a man—disabled, out of work, in trouble with his finances and facing bankruptcy—in the eyes and tell him I would "help" him for the small fee of a thousand dollars. Nor would I tell the woman, charged with driving under the influence and a Breathalyzer® reading well over the legal limit, that I would get her reduced to reckless driving for fifteen hundred dollars, knowing full well that such a promise was, at best, a slim possibility. I would not hammer out a simple will (by pressing a few keys on my computer and changing the names) and charge five or six hundred dollars.

---

2. At the time of this writing, Simpson was free. Of course, not true anymore

I'd never felt comfortable with the fee structure common to the legal profession. It works, I suppose, for the ones who can stomach it. But I could not, and that attitude provided one more reason for leaving. The Bible says that the love of money is the root of all evil; if that is so, and I believe it is, the American legal system is the trunk, limbs, leaves and seeds. For only a profound love—or perhaps, lust—of the almighty dollar could produce a fee structure that practitioners are able to quote to desperate clients without so much as a flinch.

Additionally, and it is fair to tell you this at this point, I became a father for the first time, and I knew that a legal career would make the kind of demand on my time that would likely preclude me from doing the job a father needs to do, from spending the time needed to raise the kind of kids who will be an asset to society. And hopefully not as lawyers.

If I sound like I am seething at the legal profession, it is because I am. The system of American law is a cancer, a Rube Goldberg-fashioned maze devoid of blueprint or planning, each dead-end or turn devised from a pendulum-like necessity to cure a past ill, to right a past wrong, to stop a past gap. At this stage of its "completion," those who have contributed to its construction—lawyers, judges (who are but lawyers), and legislators (again, lawyers)—afraid of the personal and professional ramifications that surely would accompany openly decrying those famous constructionists who came before them, and perhaps in love with the notion of one day becoming one, are left only to ignore the beast the law has become.

Like a near-sighted man holding the page too close to his eyes, lawyers are able to pretend the larger picture does not even exist. They will take out their microscopes and peer into the inner workings to show you the fine detail of their work, but they will not provide you with overhead pictures. They will recite mantras like, "If the glove doesn't fit, you must acquit," over and over until you forget whose glove it is, and whether there are any other reasons it might not fit. The Law is like an elephant in the living room that your mom just vacuums around, and its practitioners will scour the carpeting in search of some obscurity or technicality or absurdity to which to draw your attention until you are just plain tired of looking and you forget about the elephant altogether.

I want to be your new neighbor who enters your home and the first thing he says is, "Hey, what's with the elephant?"

I suppose there are those who will say that I am a bitter man who never achieved success in the legal field so I must be venting my frustration by writing this book. I suppose that's a possibility. What if I had become the next Gerry Spence or Ralph Nader? Would I still feel this way? While I will admit that I might not be writing this now, at this point in my life, a 42-year-old "retired" lawyer, I have to honestly say that I believe I would have written it someday anyway. After all, Ralph Nader has not made monetary hay out of his success as a consumer advocate, and Mr. Spence, while not a pauper, has given his time, energy and yes, money, towards the goal of taking the mask off the Law.

Anyway, I am writing this now, as it has been on my mind for nearly a year, percolating, festering, I guess. Whether or not it makes a difference in your life is up to you. Like I said, it's New Year's Day, year 2000. The world goes on.

We'll start by looking at law school, law students and law professors. This is not *The Paper Chase* or even Scott Turow's *One L.* You'll be surprised. Then we'll see into the world of the legal practitioner, experience the devolution of the human spirit, and how the Law, if practiced to a level of "success" as defined by a greedy society, transforms human beings into facilitators of monetary transfer and disinterested and dispirited administrators of the Criminal Code.

We'll discuss "precedent," the one-dimensional shaky foundation upon which all law is built, and see how the variety of interpretations by countless individual and self-centered judges has created a sea of aberrant "Law" that boggles the common-sense minds of the People with its nuance. We'll see how those who see fit to "interpret" the Constitution by arrogantly imputing their own modern-day spin on the well-chosen and thoughtful words of the Framers have eroded the very spirit of our nation's most cherished document, and perverted the very freedom it was intended to secure for The People.

You'll read about a variety of areas of the law and society that have been forever changed—and not in a good way—because of the hungry litigator: The First, Second, Fourth, Fifth and Sixth Amendments to the Constitution; Affirmative Action; The Right To Life. We'll look at distorted outcomes in Products Liability, Employment, and the Criminal Law.

Now and then, I'll offer words of encouragement, because at the time they will be sorely needed. You need to know that, although you live in a deeply regulated and law-saturated society, there is hope and you'll be surprised where you will find it.

Using historical case law and anecdotes from my own practice, I'll outline how the crisis-intervention nature of The Law fails (or chooses not) to foresee the pitfalls in its "logic", thereby establishing a very lucrative and secure future for her lawyers. More law equals more lawyers; more lawyers equal more law.

From time to time, I'll be unable to prevent myself from referencing the original Law, the "Mosaic" law, better known as the Ten Commandments. To me, and to many of you, these mandates, thousands of years old, provide an ageless practical framework for living the brevity of human life. However, they are filled with common sense, the vile enemy of The Law.

Mostly, I'll confirm what you already know about the Law. That is, it is a money-driven semi-transparent shroud draped over each and every facet of your life, from before you were born until after you die, deriving its only legitimacy from perpetual self-affirmation and indignantly (and with some success) trying to convince The People of its necessity. The United States is different, people say, because it is a country run by the "Rule Of Law," and not some dictator or authoritarian. Well, you be the judge.

One final note: I must separate out those legal professionals who perform services best described as an "office practice." By this I am referring to those lawyers who practice in the areas of Real Estate, Wills, Trusts and Estates, Intellectual Property and lawyers who draft Contracts and Partnership Agreements and establish Corporations. These lawyers operate in relative isolation from the so-called "litigators," who take actual cases to courts and cause all the trouble. Additionally, I'm going to do an awful lot of generalizing in this book. I'll have to clarify now that I know there exist people who are part of these general groups who defy those generalizations, who do not fit the mold of the group. That's the fact in any generalization, isn't it? Whether you are the exception or the mother of an exception or just happen to know somebody who's the exception to the generalization, it is unnecessary to contact me to tell me so.

By the way, if you are the exception, I thank you for your honest service. We're all very proud of you.

A Lifetime of The Law

The United States has drifted away from the Founders' concept of "We The People" to a nation gripped by the rule of Law. Nearly everything we do on a daily basis from *before* the day we are born falls under the cloud of The Law. Worse than that, in the past several decades The Law has deputized us into a legion of civil litigants and pseudo-prosecutors who have been conditioned to seek legal retribution for every conceivable wrongdoing of another. But, the Law is a shaky house of cards poorly constructed and self-affirmed by her well-paid practitioners, whose goal (under the guise of "helping people") is to stir the pot of dispute amongst The People and feed the greedy monster called "The Law," and to line the pockets of her lawyers.

Think about it. Before you are born, the Law is there. First, to decide upon whether you even *will* be born or not. The Law has dominion over that. Then, the doctor who oversees your birth and hospital where you are born are regulated by licensing requirements, which are accompanied by educational requirements, both of which are mandates of the law. Additionally, the doctor and hospital and all of the medical personnel associated with your birth are overseen by a huge insurance conglomerate regulated by the Law, and, God forbid, if something should go wrong during your birth, the Law and a cadre of lawyers will seek out legal punishments and remedies in retribution and retaliation for that wrong.

When you make it into the world, if you live in the United States your parents will be required by law to, on occasion, have your body penetrated by toxic and poisonous sera, ostensibly to inoculate you against ancient diseases known to have had devastating and epidemic effects upon the population. The Law requires it. When your parents drop you off at a daycare provider, you can be sure that that provider has undergone legal scrutiny and complied with a variety of regulations and licensing requirements thanks to the Law. When you go to school—whether public or private—that institution and its teachers and administrators have met educational and licensing requirements mandated by law, and the teachers are usually represented by a labor union which works to negotiate the pay and benefit packages with the school board, all of which are functions of the Law.

As a student, you will be required to satisfy certain educational requirements in order to progress through your education and, eventually, graduate. Those requirements are mandated by Law. To get a driver's license and own a car, you must comply with the Law, which, in every state, requires that you maintain a certain amount of liability insurance on the vehicle.

If you choose to continue your education, again, the requirements for both students and professors are handed down by the ever-present Law. Nearly every career you may wish to enter has certain educational and licensing requirements.

To buy a house requires adherence to stiff legal standards. The area of real estate is bursting with Law; the transfer of legal title, acquiring and qualifying for financing, even strict supervision of the real estate professionals who broker the deal. And the house you buy? It's been built to a plethora of structural and safety standards called "Building Code," and only after the builder purchased a construction permit, all mandated by Law.

Want to travel abroad? Get ready for another round of inoculations, not to mention a background check for that passport so that you may re-enter the United States when your traveling days are over.

As you move into your working days, the Law watches over every part of employment. It requires that you are paid a certain minimum amount of money per hour, that your workplace adheres to a plethora of safety and environmental standards, that your employer walks a tightrope between the needs of his business and the Law. He must keep a very strict accounting of your pay—so that, at the end of the pay period he can withhold a percentage of *your money* to send into the Federal Government to pay for statutorily created welfare like unemployment insurance, Social Security and Medicare, not to mention the completely unconstitutional Federal Income Tax.

If you're lucky, your employer will assist you in preparing for your retirement by matching payroll contributions to retirement plans like a 401(k)[3]. That number is not an arbitrary number; it is a section in the Federal Code pertaining to the IRS,[4] comprising some 25 pages of text. That's one law.

One day, you might get married. Although already God-ordained (a marriage between a man and a woman, anyway), the Law feels the need to make it all legal. That arrogance isn't free, either. Alas, with the divorce rate exceeding fifty percent, you may one day choose to dissolve your marriage. A matrimonial lawyer will collect all the information as well as a financial statement, ostensibly to determine how the marital assets will be divided. Of course, armed with that information, he or she will know intimately how many billable hours to expend

---

3. I know, I know...but someday these plans might be healthy again.
4. In fact, TITLE 26 Subtitle A CHAPTER 1 Subchapter D PART I Subpart A § 401.

on your case, and either you or your spouse (or both) will end up paupers. Too often, of course, marital dissolution eviscerates the financial resources of the husband. More importantly, two people who once loved one another often become bitter enemies, thanks to the adversarial nature of the law invading such a personal relationship

Upon retirement (which, by the way, is *legally mandatory* in many professions) the Law dictates further. If you take your Social Security retirement benefits, the Law tells you how much money you can earn over and above that pittance in order to keep receiving your payments (unless you're a congressman, in which case the Social Security administration is not part of your life whatsoever). As you age, if you wish to keep driving you will have to comply with more frequent testing to insure you are physically able to operate a motor vehicle (unless you live in Florida, where I have witnessed a customer in my barbershop consume *nine minutes* to get from his vehicle, parked right in front of the shop, to the barber chair).

Eventually, you will die. You'd think that'd be the end of it, right? Well, it physically is, for you anyway. But your *estate* lives on. Money you owe, monies owed you, any partnership agreements you may have been in, any real estate you may have owned, all your personal property and the like, will be handled inside the confines of your estate. If you do not have a will,[5] the Law has decided that a significant portion of your accumulated wealth and possessions belong to the State in which you die. In fact, the only good thing, legally speaking, that comes from your death is in a case where you happen to be under indictment for a criminal charge; usually the prosecutor will drop the charges when you die. Usually.

---

5 .A Will is an essential document, readily available and inexpensive these days.

This life you've lived, even if completely devoid of any events that bring you to the unhappy specter of the Law—things like lawsuits or criminal charges—was always under the watchful eye of several governmental authorities who owe their legitimacy to the Law. The Law, enacted by our own representatives purportedly acting in our best interests and, again *purportedly*, within the confines of the United States Constitution, enforced by a legion of dedicated public servants and interpreted by a cadre of unaccountable judicial professionals, runs our lives.

I don't think that's what the Framers had in mind.

The all-encompassing nature and presence of the Law in our lives has a chilling effect on freedom, creativity, commerce, and the natural order of life itself. Our relationships—whether they be within the confines of our own homes or the workplace or any other public arena—are scrutinized and dissected by elitists who feel the need to meddle in those relationships. These powerful and oppressive individuals, believing themselves to be specially gifted with insight and knowledge far surpassing that of the rank and file citizenry, are called "lawyers," and, when conglomerated together, "The Law."

As the United States has matured, the Law has grown into a multi-headed hydra, sprawling across the country and her People seemingly without direction or form. Like a huge prehistoric meteor from space, the Law has left a huge impact upon us all. But unlike that meteor, the Law's impact has happened over time, eroding the fabric of freedom like a river flowing in all directions. Its movement has been so subtle that few have even noticed.

A frog is placed in a beaker of water over a small flame. After a while, the frog is comfortable, the warming of the water keeping its systems moving and feeling good. Two days later, the frog is poached to death.

That's how the Law got us all.
And it's not over yet.

WHO ARE THESE LAWYERS?

I don't think I ever would have gone to law school if it hadn't been for my parents. Now, if you were my parents, you would find that statement odd, indeed. My parents—with whom I have had little real contact since an autumn day in 1975 when I bid them farewell and boarded an airplane bound for Cape May, New Jersey, home of the Eastern United States Recruit Training Center for the United States Coast Guard— never mentioned law school once. Never did they mention medical school, or any professional school for that matter. For very low-income people who were happy to have gas in the car and thawed water pipes, a son with a regular paper route is successful. Had I followed through with my plans to attend college and ultimately teach music in high school, I would have completely upset the balance in the "dysfunctional poster family."

You see, it's okay to want to be more than your father, as long as it's not *much* more. A step, maybe two, okay. But college? Music? Why, who do you think you are? What's wrong with blue-collar work? Are you too good for an honest day's work? Huh?? And *music?* Well, there's no future in music!

And you could understand some of it if I was a bad kid. I suppose I had been a handful. Voted King of the Winter Carnival my senior year of high school, voted most improved in music over the four years of high school (I had taught myself to play several instruments during high school), co-captain of the Varsity Hockey team, asked to direct the concert band at graduation, accolades after accolades for community service. I was popular, and I was dedicated to music. Alas, my grades were ghastly.

Despite the favor shown me by my classmates and many, many others in our little community of Gardiner, Maine, my parents never seemed to notice me. I don't know if it was jealousy, or just that they didn't understand or approve of my value system, such as it was. They could not control me and so it was away to the military.

And they might not admit it to your face, but Mom and Dad were glad to see me go. Let me tell you now that it makes little difference if thousands, or hundreds of thousands, or millions of people love you or approve of you or wish they were you or at least *knew* you; if your parents do not like you, you feel like a failure. Like you let somebody down. Like you have no value.

And you will do anything to try to win them over, including becoming an *Attorney At Law.*

Anyway, I look back over the years since I walked away from the instability of my insufficient upbringing and see that, no matter how far I travel from my parents—whether one is to judge it in terms of miles or decades—I'm still trying to win their favor, or, at the very least, get their attention.[6]

You're thinking: *This guy's crazy.*

Well, reports differ.

I just had to take a moment of your time to give you some idea of how one man came to be a lawyer. (*I could have said, "decided to," or "chose to," but each relies too heavily upon, at least, a modicum of control, of which I had none.*) Because, in order to understand the law, you must understand her lawyers. After

---

6. Actually, Dad passed away in 2002.

all, without the life-blood of the life-blood*less*, the law would just lie there like a sheep on its back, flailing its legs until it just died of starvation and thirst.

So, why did I go to law school?

As I made my way through college, I realized that I had the opportunity to be anything I wanted to be. My brother had already begun his legal career at Northeastern Law School, and I guess I figured if he could do it, so could I. After all, I was smart, and I always loved to argue. Like a lot of people, I always root for the underdog. I thought I wanted to be a David in what I saw as a sea of Goliaths. Additionally, I was fired from a nice job with a large corporation, and wanted to learn how to never let that happen again, to me or anybody else.

But there was one incident in my young adult years that may have provided the impetus for my legal career.

I was 17, driving home from my girlfriend's house—late. I had the Polara up to about 70 MPH when Gardiner Police Officer Brian McMaster came up from behind, blue lights flashing.

I got the ticket, but I was driving on my probationary license and I knew that meant I'd lose my license for 30 days.

When I went to court, I got fined, but I was never asked for my license. I figured I'd dodged a bullet.

After graduation, I was working full-time at the Howard Johnson's Restaurant on the Turnpike when the letter arrived, demanding I send my license in for 30 days. To me, that didn't seem right, waiting until Summer to execute this law.

Well, Dad took me up to the DMV, and we began with one of the clerks, where we got absolutely no help. Then to the director of the Maine Division of Motor Vehicles (this was back when a person could actually speak to these authority figures). Nothing. Up the hill to our legislator's office. He wasn't in. We went from office to office, up the chain of command until we were in the Attorney General's office. He *actually* met with us. Alas, he could not help. Around the corner was the Lieutenant Governor's office, and we walked right in, Dad as adamant as me. I don't even remember who was the Lieutenant Governor, but he, while sympathetic and probably in need of a vote next election, could not change the law.

The Governor was out of town.

But as my Dad and I walked with purpose around the State Capitol, it occurred to me that we needed somebody to fight for us, somebody to go to bat for us in a battle for what we saw as a miscarriage of justice. I guess maybe, as an adult, that guy could be me.

I also loved to write. Dr. Jeff Rackham, my faculty advisor at the University of North Carolina at Asheville, was dumbfounded when I told him I was thinking about law school. He shook his head and looked at me as though he was seeing me for the first time.

"*Law* school? Why do you want to do that to yourself?" is what I think he said. He was incredulous, as though I had just told him I was thinking of joining a cult.

I bristled at his reaction; who was this guy, and why would he say such a thing about the law? I respected him and admired him; unfortunately, not enough to give his objection any thought.

I didn't understand or even comprehend my motivation while it was happening to me; I thought I wanted to stand up in front of juries and argue for mercy and expose the fatal flaw in my opposition's case. I thought I wanted to go to bat for those who could not, or would not, go to bat for themselves. Ha! How big of an ego can a person have?

In those moments in brief discussion with Dr. Rackham, my true colors came shining through; I was on the defensive immediately, and in those few seconds I made up my mind to let nothing stand in the way of my quest to become a lawyer. That indignant stance, built upon a milky gray foundation, unearthed in me the irrational arrogance that, as it turns out, is the unsubstantial platform upon which many lawyers stand.

Most lawyers are so thoroughly narcissistic and out of touch with the rank and file citizenry that they don't know how to even *talk* to it.

Case in point:

I worked closely with a lawyer in Florida on some (yawn) eminent domain matters. Eminent Domain is the right of the government to "take" private property for public purposes, as long as "just compensation" is paid to the owner.[7] The law of Eminent Domain emerged as a very important component to the Bill of Rights (enumerated in the Fifth Amendment thereto), and in response to the British Crown's nasty habit of just *taking* what they needed. Imperialism brought about manifest destiny which brought taking. The Framers thought that was wrong, but not out of the question. So, they allowed public takings but required "just compensation."

And your question and mine and everybody's question is, "what's just?" Well, of course it's different for everybody. Which means a court must decide which means there must be at least three lawyers involved which is just one of the reasons I'm writing this book.

---

7 As recently as 2007, the United States Supreme Court ruled in favor of a governmental agency's right to take private property for the sole public purpose of increasing tax revenue. *Kelo v. City of New London, 545 U.S. 469.* In response, every state in the union enacted legislation prohibiting Eminent Domain actions where the sole public purpose is to increase tax revenue.

However, Eminent Domain, in the modern context, usually means that the Department of Transportation (DOT) comes in and slices off a chunk of your front yard to widen a street. As populations increase and traffic with them, widening streets to handle the volume of traffic has to be considered a "public purpose." But, Eminent Domain can also mean that the government decides that citrus canker, a highly contagious virus that attacks orange trees, needs to be contained by the contamination or "condemnation" of your orange grove somewhere in central Florida. The State Agriculture commission comes in and decides what is "just" and offers you that much so they can destroy your trees. As you may guess, the amount is never remotely enough to compensate you for your loss, including your loss of future income from that grove, and so you go to court. And, that means money, from a legal standpoint anyway. Just one minimal case like I described above can require several lawyers, half a dozen experts, surveys, plans, estimates, appraisals. The kicker (in Florida and many other jurisdictions) is that the expert's and lawyer's fees are required by statute to be paid by the government (actually the "condemning authority" or whomever wants your property), which means you and me and every other taxpayer. What can and does happen, more often than not, is something like this:

A homeowner is approached by, say, the County, and it wants to widen the street in front of a homeowner's house. It has already done some estimating and appraisals of its own—very minimal, mind you, government dollars at work—and, let's say the County offers this homeowner $4,000 for a permanent easement four feet wide and 75 feet long along the front of his property. The homeowner may decide that it's a good deal, and is ready to accept. That's when a duty-driven lawyer's letter arrives at his door saying, "WAIT!! DON'T SIGN ANY-

THING UNTIL YOU CHECK WITH A LAWYER AND SEE IF YOU'RE GETTING THE *FULL VALUE* FOR YOUR PROPERTY." The letter is expertly drafted, accompanied by the lawyer's resume and a list of satisfied clients, and ensures no cost to the homeowner. Our homeowner bites.

He retains this lawyer who commences the process of:

Hiring an expert real estate appraiser – Minimum: $5,000;

Hiring an accountant – Minimum - $500;

Hiring a Land Surveyor – Minimum $150;

Ordering the jobsite plans, as well as copies of all documents – Minimum $80.

Our lawyer bills out at $200 per hour and has a secretary and Paralegal who bill out at $100 per hour, collectively.

Now, after it is all said and done—after our lawyer has put the County's feet to the fire—the County comes back with a new offer of $7,500 for the property, and our lawyer recommends our homeowner take it. Never mind that it has been fifteen months since the original offer and our homeowner cannot sell his home with the cloud of impending severance overhanging it. Our lawyer bills for about a hundred hours, and half that for his staff. All the experts are paid and the total is somewhere in the neighborhood of $30,720 to the taxpayers, for property worth around $4,000. Most of that money goes to, you guessed, the lawyer.

I worked closely with one lawyer on many of these cases. His whole schpiel revolved around "getting the full value of your property." Right. He has convinced himself that he is providing a vital service to property owners. He is the civil public defender.

Anyway, this guy, a real neo-Nazi type, was such a racist that even he didn't know it. All he knew was that he was somehow better than lots of "clueless" people, especially people of color.

I sat in on a meeting between him and several women from a couple of black families who owned property adjacent to a major interstate highway job. I heard him consistently talk down to them, sometimes actually speaking louder as if they were deaf, and refer to them over and over as "you guys." A room full of women! Even while looking at the prospect of lengthy litigation involving a $4 million taking, he had no inclination to attempt to see the world from their point of view. He once confided to me that he skipped an entire class one college semester because the professor joshed him about his name. How thin-skinned and small-minded does one have to be to become a lawyer? (Well, we'll get to that in a moment). That's just one lawyer, one in a sea of passive-aggressive nit-pickers, hell-bent on paying society back for being bullied on the playground or that "kick me" sign some kid stealthily affixed to his back. I'm not at all kidding.

"But, Wendell, aren't lawyers picked from the best and the brightest of the best academia circles? And aren't they driven by some greater sense of greater good for society? And, don't they want to help people?" you ask.

In order to understand law students, one must understand law schools. Law schools are profit making institutions. Period. If you've got an undergraduate degree from somewhere, *anywhere*, you can get a law degree. No, not necessarily from Harvard or Stanford, or any one of the other hundred or so "plum" law schools in the country. But there are schools, lots of institutes of higher learning, that have an accredited law school, where nearly anybody, okay forget 'nearly', *anybody* can get a law degree. Right now, in the United States, there are more law *students* than there are law*yers*. Great, huh?

Now, law schools must maintain a somewhat satisfactory level of bar passage, that is, students who graduate must be able, by and large, to pass the bar exam. (Later, we'll discuss how this really happens). But in today's society with a seemingly endless variety of career paths one in possession of a law degree may choose, not all law school graduates even sit for the bar exam. Many students are only interested in an understanding of the law in order to bolster or assist them in their other career objectives, such as an MBA or a Cosmetic Surgeon. So, if a hundred students graduate and 65 pass the bar, that may seem like an unacceptable level of education. However, law schools simply argue that, while a few of the remaining students didn't pass, the rest simply didn't *wish* to pass. Once a law school has been around a while, no accrediting board takes a very serious look at passage rates anymore, unless they get ridiculously out of kilter.

Then there is the question of lineage and legacy. *My grandfather graduated from Harvard Law, my father graduated from Harvard Law, I graduated from Harvard Law…*so where do you think the daughter is going to law school? What say, for instance, she's really not that bright? Yep, she's been to all the correct prep schools and the finest finishing schools money can buy. But let's just say she's a dolt. Think that has any bearing whatsoever on her future?

Now, let's clarify. Many bright individuals have entered and graduated from Harvard Law School, and many have gone on to be important and valued members of the bar. Many graduates who have no money or lengthy ties to Harvard Law School have been quite successful as well. I'm only illustrating the point that "best and brightest" is not always the case.

Oh, let's talk about the "best and the brightest" for a minute.

How does one get to be the best and the brightest, do you suppose? And what exactly does that mean? There are, I figure, two ways.

First, a person can go to college and have the time of his or her life, partying, playing, shirking, skipping classes, you name it. Then, when it comes time to take exams or hand in papers, that individual can really cram, cram his or her hand down into the wallet and retrieve sufficient cash to procure the test answers or papers or projects that will garner the student a top grade. It happens all the time, especially in the Greek micro-society, and at least some of these "best and brightest" go on to become lawyers, doctors, airplane pilots, senators, congresspersons and presidents. Believe it.

Second, one can spend hour after hour of his or her spare time in a library or at home locked away in a room studying, reading, making notes, completely absorbed in the passivity of learning. In so doing, he or she misses out on all that life has to offer outside of the cocoon. More dangerous, I believe, is that he or she can become so dependent upon the written word that it takes on a certain self-proving characteristic, rendering critical-thinking skills, the kind that often accompany social and cultural interaction and progress (not to mention fair-minded problem solving), unnecessary.

Cursed with the single-minded motivation to win at any cost (wonder how they got that way?), they have often overlooked a great deal of what adolescence is supposed to teach. They will occasionally pack up with like-minded students, if only to bolster their fragile esteem by pointing and snickering and slapping each other on the back and pulling each other's fingers. It is pre-historic or primordial or just plain stupid, but it is the price they pay, not for genius, but for the *grades*.

The best and the brightest are nothing unless they have the *grades* to prove it. In an academic society absent grades, they are but a herd of children in adult bodies who may accidentally know a lot. We call them the "best and the brightest" based solely upon their *grades*! They study and cram and worry and think and the paranoia mounts and the weight begins to fall off or pack on and the fingernails are missing and the Mountain Dew is bought by the twelve-pack. The test comes, and the answers spill out like the lunches of rookie cruise-ship passengers, and the test goes. And they have succeeded. They have the *grades* to prove it. They have withdrawn their Excalibur from the stone and they will hold it high to show of just what they are made. But Arthur was just a weak little boy cursed by sorcery, destined to become the king ultimately undone by jealousy and his own uncontrollable madness.

These people are your law students.

And let's talk a bit about that old "helping people" stuff.

Never let it be said that I am completely cynical about the motivation of law students. Of course there are those who see a distant and greater calling on their lives, a gut-wrenching inability to open their mouths and accept like trusting baby birds the gruel that is life. They are proactive, and they are driven, and they are able to "make a difference." They point to the likes of JFK and Oliver Wendell Holmes and Sandra Day O'Connor and Martin Luther King and say, "They believed in their causes, and they made a difference, and so can I."

And you have to believe that it is possible. Heck, I've said for a long time that the most difficult aspect of being successful is determining what it is that you want to do with your life. However, due to the extreme of the forces placed on our lives as we mature, our notions of what it is that we actually want compared to what it is that society influences us into *believing* we want, we often make bad choices. And those bad choices can often lead to outcomes we never believed possible: Unhappiness, poor performance, ignorance and apathy, the feeling of being trapped, low self-esteem, and surrender.

The reason we make the bad choices is often caused by our lack of proper investigation into the pathway we've chosen. For instance, we might look into the sky and see the Blue Angels, The United States Navy Air Demonstration Team, zinging fifty feet above the treetops at four-hundred knots and then see the crowd, mouths open in awe, and then see the pilots exiting the planes after the show and marching together to give out autographs and we might conclude that we want to fly a jet. Or, we might go to a major league baseball game and watch the long-ballers or the hard-throwing pitchers, or the gymnastics of the center-fielder robbing a batter of a home run, and see the crowd reaction, and decide, 'yes, that's what I want to be.' Or maybe you go to a concert and hear the music and see the girls going ga-ga over the performer and want that life.

Without thorough investigation into these career fields, one can end up very unhappy. Unhappy because of the sacrifices he or she has to make to achieve that kind of "success." Unhappy because of the lack of raw talent that prevents the rise to the "big leagues." Unhappy because of the pace, or the monotony, or whatever you didn't see going in.

Or maybe you become disillusioned because the people you wanted to help don't want your help. Or because you didn't see that the act of helping one necessarily hurts another.

And that's the way it is in the law. Helping one person or one entity translates into hurting another. That is the nature of the law. Lawyers, civil lawyers anyway, are merely facilitators of monetary transfers. And so, after years of undergraduate school and three years of crusading in law school, bleeding-heart lawyers go into the world and take the cases of the down-trodden and the poor and the stupid people who make stupid mistakes. And they take the cases until the light goes and it occurs to them that "helping others" is merely a euphemism for "hurting others," and they decide as long as that's the way it is, they will start looking for the *rich* stupid people and rep-resent them. The entire process takes but a few years, but it does happen. And, when that happens, you could look into a crowd of lawyers and be completely unable to distinguish the kind-hearted of the "best and the brightest" from the rest. If that sounds cynical to you, remember that I *am* one of them. In the last analysis, you must remember that, like a stockbro-ker or a bookie, a lawyer's job is to make sure that large sums of money transfer from one hand to another, stopping in the middle to offload a significant portion of it to the "best and the brightest." Ultimately, the "from" and "to" are not important; the stop in the middle is the only thing that counts.

Helping people, while a noble and worthy endeavor, is one that cannot be accomplished in the hallowed halls of "justice." And those who attempt it often walk away, heads shaking in disbelief, realizing that "success" in the practice of law requires only one essential characteristic: To be acutely able to ignore the elephant in the living room.

Maybe you are a lawyer and you're reading this. Maybe you don't see it that way at all. That's your prerogative. I've no doubt that, given sufficient resources, you could formulate a decent enough argument to shoot down everything I've said up to now. That's what you get paid to do, and you better find a way to win the argument, son, or it's off the fast track to partnership. If we were in court, I'm sure that you would find a way to exclude much of what I've said up to now such that a jury would only get to really decide upon what it is *you* have said and decide that I'm just a raving lunatic with a chip on his shoulder. Well, that is the law, isn't it? The law simply winnows out all that is honest and just and true in order to arrive at a ridiculous and irrational outcome that provides no real solution, but certainly works toward fostering ill will among the People. Oh, and toward beefing up the legal fees, can't forget that one.

Well, I'm only a little sorry for the likes of you. My only real hope is that you will see the light one day. If you're at all like many of my friends in the law, you are already looking for an exit, but are simply trapped into a life that requires your continued employ as an attorney at law. Maybe you're in debt up to your ears. Nice house, fancy car, place at the lake, country club membership, private schooling for the kids, etc. Gotta keep the bucks flowing in to keep up that appearance. Or, maybe you're really an idiot who simply cannot do anything but slice up words and hammer the metal law into the shape you want in order to win the argument of the day. Maybe you just can't bear the thought of being known as something other than "esquire."

But still it gnaws at you. I know it does. Way down deep where you won't talk about at all, you wonder what it must be like to go bankrupt, or be in the unenviable position of having to plead to something you didn't do just to avoid the maximum punishment. You have a *feeling* that millions and millions of big tobacco dollars in your pocket just doesn't seem right, given that the plaintiff smoked of his own volition for thirty years.

Well, that may be how it is if you're a lawyer reading this (bravo, by the way, for continuing this far). But you have to realize that many people are not lawyers. Some simply because they choose not to be. And they are reading this right now, and nodding their heads along with these words because they know—they *know*—without it being proclaimed from the bench or the jury box that I'm onto something here. A wise man once said, and I'll paraphrase here, once you hear a truth it is like you have known it all your life. There is something liberating about the truth, something that keeps sane people sane in the face of insane judgments, and unfair acquittals. It isn't much, I'll grant you. But it is enough to keep us from killing one another.

Or is it?

Take a look around you. Whether in traffic or on the television, or at a pee-wee hockey game. People are lashing out at one another—physically, I'm saying—at an alarming rate. People are choosing to go to blows over stuff that used to get us a little hot under the collar, but now sends us right over the edge.

Now, here's my theory: People are overwhelmed by the emotions they are feeling regarding the injustice in the world such that, when they are affected or impacted by a perhaps minor injustice, all the emotion and frustration they are feeling is multiplied to the point of loss of self-control. Add to that the visions of violence bombarding from all directions, and the limitations of civility, or the boundaries to common decency and restraint are enlarged or moved outward to the point where simple assault against one with whom we disagree no longer seems uncalled for or overreacting. Call it vigilantism descended, or something like that. Now it's not an angry mob going after a horse thief, it's an enraged parent attacking a hockey coach, or an angry neighbor "settling" a difference over an overhanging limb. Or, sadly, a husband feeding his low self-esteem by beating his once-adored wife.

And the lawyers love it. They so love the fact that people are at odds with one another that disputes arise over the pettiest of valueless subjects. They love it because that is what keeps them in business. Over 70,000 in Florida alone! Sheesh, I could still be one of them. As long as there are lawyers, there will be pain and suffering. To nurture grievances until they become full-blown, billable disputes is the call of every lawyer. It's the same reason four out of five dentists recommend toothpaste loaded with sugar, or why antacids cause stomach problems.

Crisis intervention is who we are. A handful of religious fanatics in the Motherland were savvy enough to see the handwriting on the wall, to see the other religious fanatics tightening the gauntlet around them so much that they loaded themselves into a rickety little boat and pushed off, headed God knows where. I mean, you think the Pilgrims really had a *plan*? They were running away from tyranny, no different from the boatloads of Cuban families who would rather risk drowning in the Florida straits than to wait around for "the goodbye look." It's not so much going *to* a better life as it is running *from* an unbearable one, and it is the thread at the very core of American human existence.

The law itself is established for the sole purpose of crisis intervention. After the fact. The effect to the cause. Do this, and this will happen. Kill and you get this punishment. Injure another and you pay this. The law is not at all about prevention. Nowhere in the canons or casebooks or Reporters does anybody ever forward a plan to *prevent* the need for the intervention of the legal system. "It is not," I'm sure they will say, "our job." That's like the mechanic who fixes your car changing the oil without changing the filter. And it is that blatant irresponsibility that enables the lawyer to completely disregard the human ramifications of what he or she achieves so long as it satisfies the criteria: Uphold The Law. Beyond that, the example that is set is simply this: Somebody Else Is To Blame.

How many times have you heard something like, "Well, you may not like it but it's the law"? Or how about, "Well, it's not perfect, but it's the best system in the world"? Those are mealy-mouthed excuses in a country where the buck never stops. You know why people love those old Perry Mason shows? Because there were those great scenes where the seasoned lawyer would be mercilessly grilling a witness on the stand, badgering, testifying, asking question on top of question (by the way, no opposing counsel or judge would ever let another lawyer get away with any of that in real life), until either the witness or somebody in the gallery jumped to his or her feet to exclaim, "Alright, I did it!!". That cathartic moment, that exhilarating, room-clearing, waterfall of truth is so beautiful. It's the peace when your newborn finally cries himself back to sleep at 3 AM. What remains is clarity, clarity of mind and of the air and of your vision. What remains is what was once there, a solid and comfortable belief, no, no, a *knowledge* that there is a truth, and when the layers of deceit are dusted away there it is, shiny and unscratched and pure.

The people are crying out, day after deceit-filled day, for somebody to stand up and take responsibility. I was driving the other day, exiting a business parking lot where the entrance and exit were divided by a small median. As I approached the exit, a car entering the lot disregarded the median and entered through the exit side, right in front of me. Although not in any danger of a collision at the slow speed, he cut me off. I really was about to give it nothing more than a "well, there's another moron," when the guy stopped, turned back to me and waved a hand. "Totally sorry, man," he called out. "My fault completely."

"No problem," I returned. But something happened to me in that moment. Something that happens occasionally, and the rush of "feelgoodness" in me is overwhelming and can buoy me for days. The simple act of another human taking responsibility for something as mundane as a traffic miscue has that kind of power in me. He took a comb and pulled straight the locks of a tangled web of a self-serving throng of uncaring individuals and refreshed my faith in human nature (join hands and sing "We Are The World"). Sicky sweet? If you say so. I say it's the missing ingredient in a world made up of people.

And lawyers prey upon it. Why? Only because it is profitable to do so. The Golden Rule is so simple, but it does have a "chicken and the egg" kind of dilemma attached to it. "Do unto others as you would have others do unto you." The problem is, we forget who "you" is, if you will. You is *you*. People want to back into the Golden Rule, to use it as a retaliatory device. "Well, so and so did this to me, so he must want that kind of treatment back." Uh-uh. It doesn't work in that direction. It begins and ends with "you." There is an implied "you" at the beginning, as in *"you* do unto others..."

Some have perverted the Golden Rule, saying, "Do unto others *before* they do unto you." These are cynical, insecure people who are certain the world is out to get them. They feel that they deserve to live a life without pain or worry or problems, and may have been "victimized" by the everyday acts of an uncaring neighbor. Many of them are lawyers. My belief is that these people would not feel that way if there were truth, if there were justice. If there were more people in their lives who said, "sorry, man."

You see, the law was really invented as a great big "sorry, man." Saying "I'm sorry" isn't always enough. I've said that to my kids when they do something really egregious and then say "I'm sorry daddy." To that I say, "Well, sorry doesn't cut it this time." There has to be a punishment, a retribution. They have to have something to remember the depth of their transgression, ostensibly to prevent recidivism.[8]

But the original Law, the Ten Commandments, only laid it down. It said, "Thou shall not..." and left out the "or else." It was up to the society to establish the "or else," and establish we did. Of course, we did so within the confines of a Constitution, but that never prevented the quick and clean legal system called "vigilantism."

I meet people every day who are disgusted with the ridiculous appeals system, the one that keeps condemned killers out of the gas chamber for a dozen years or more. It is an age-old struggle of what life is worth. Will you pay for a condemned killer's room and board (and education and appeals and special diet and and and) for twenty years until he has exhausted the legal system?

As mortals, we are uniquely unqualified to make that judgment. We each bring to the table an immense amount of paradox, and the balancing act we try to perform makes us look like a bear on a bicycle. Unfortunately, all too often in such an environment our emotions drive our decisions.

And our emotions are driven by so many different events. The nature of the homicide, the degree of deviance—and remorse—exhibited by the killer, and the identity of the victim all figure in to our decision. Be honest, one drug dealer kills another and almost nobody cares. (Why the police with whom I am acquainted don't dance with glee when this happens is beyond me, but they all, to a person, simply cannot condone any kind of crime). But a sex weirdo strangles a seven-year-old boy with his underwear after having his way with him, and we all go nuts. We see pictures of the kid in his baseball uniform

---

8. Fancy word for "repeat offenders".

and sporting a toothy grin all over the television and we want only a tall tree and a short rope. I'm right. That's the way God intended. His Son, Jesus, said that children were special in His eyes, and that anybody who hurts a child would be better off if a millstone were tied to his neck and he were tossed into the depths of the sea.

But the law doesn't see it that way.

The law, they say, is blind. The law, they say, isn't law unless it's applied exactly the same across the board. So the drug dealer gets a lawyer and the sex weirdo gets a lawyer and before you know it, they've pled out and the sentences are plied out in such a manner that neither will spend a significantly long time in prison. Now, I say this having not been sentenced to prison, but knowing full well that 25 years is not much to a 30 year old man. No matter what the sentence, there are some to whom it will never be enough, and some to whom it will always be too much.

And that's why there is a law in the first place. Again, the problem isn't the existence of the law; it is the existence of her mortal practitioners, and their love and zest for money and power that has perverted what justice there could have been.

Now, what about the professors who teach the "black letter law" to these future lawyers? Aren't they the "best and the brightest?" Well, for the most part, legal "scholars" are just theorists. Few have actually practiced even a minute of law. Maybe that surprises you, maybe not. Their job is to lay down the tried and true nuts and bolts of the law in its purest form (i.e. nothing at all like law in the real world). Using the famous law-changing cases (i.e. the ones the Supreme Court has heard and used to "interpret" the U.S. Constitution), Law Professors teach future lawyers the basics, all the while trying to get students to "think like a lawyer."

Law professors—having seen movies like *The Paper Chase*—know full well the fear and apprehension of the incoming law student, and they relish the opportunity to exploit those emotions. Utilizing the Socratic Method,[9] law professors select students at random or according to a seating chart to set forth the facts of the case being discussed. Then the fun begins. Professors will play devil's advocate and continue to pepper even the most prepared student with question after question, laying theoretical gibberish on top of hypothetical nightmare and never coming close to something resembling an answer. Of course, each professor has his or her own take on the Socratic Method.

One professor I had must have made some kind of deal with herself to never, *never* give a straight answer.

"Professor, I'm working the argument on this case and I've got a pretty good handle on the facts and law, and I was kind of wondering what you think about XYZ?"

She would cross her arms and look you in the eye and say the same thing: "Well, what do *you* think?"

"Well, I *know* what *I* think, I was just sort of figuring that, since you're my teacher and all, you might share your thoughts."

"Well, what are *your* thoughts?" To her, it was just a game.

I remain convinced that that particular professor had no clue what I was even talking about.

That's just one.

---

9. An interrogative engagement with one student, using questions designed to probe deeply into a given subject, purportedly to expose the deep philosophical issues contained therein, but also to embarrass and harass students.

One professor delighted in raising his voice louder than yours when you hit a nerve, when you touched upon a point that he had never even considered before.

One professor was a crazy old coot who was widely revered as the Father Of Pure Comparative Fault, and issued so many crazy and outlandish analogies that one student kept a running journal of them that filled several yellow sheets.

One professor, a young stud of a professor, enjoyed staring at the variety of young female students in his class as he spoke what he was sure were wise double entendres.

One professor, I kid you not, wore the same clothes to school every day of the entire semester. Not the same *kind* of clothes. The Same Clothes. Okay, okay, he changed his tie now and then. It was so absurd that this guy drove to school everyday in a car that looked like a bottle of Avon cologne, and got out of it in the same outfit. I had an idea.

On the last day of class—I kid you not—every one of the 80-odd students in his class dressed in *exactly the same outfit*. Imagine 80 men and women in khaki pants, a blue dress shirt, a blue blazer with gold buttons and a diagonally striped tie. The kicker? The man thought it was *flattery!*

These are the teachers of the law, teaching students of the law, who will one day be practitioners of the law.

Most are immature, insecure and frightened to death of failure, taught their "craft" by others who've convinced themselves of their own genius, and jettisoned into an ever expanding gas-filled bubble perpetually floating over the rest of us. There, they pretend to be "impartial," representing "without passion or prejudice," and remaining eternally vigilant lest someone catch on.

Believe me, a lawyer is no job for a human being.

Rule No. 1. Never Take A Stand

It takes a lot to be able to spend one's entire day lying to him or her self. It demands a certain characteristic, or cluster of them, to be consistently inconsistent, saying one thing out of one side of your mouth all the while knowing full well you will soon be betraying it from the other, amazing yourself with your ability to waffle on the issues to the clients, the other lawyers. You take sides one minute and pull a first class Benedict Arnold the next, all in the name of "lawyering." I don't think anybody has ever really dealt with the notion that lawyers really are people who simply get so caught up in the business of lawyering that they forget about being people.

And I'm not either. Lawyers become judges who wield all sorts of power and hand down all sorts of punishment and find little of forgiveness in executing their "duty." They rarely lend any serious weight to mitigating circumstances or excuse conduct based upon one's history or set of unique circumstances. If lawyers wish to sit upon the throne of justice they have created, and are content with accepting heinous amounts of money from desperate clients who haven't a chance of receiving "justice," then they have no right to expect that I will consider their unique circumstances or experiences in criticizing them. After all, the same lawyer who one day fights for the life of a client will have no trouble whatsoever condemning that same individual if that is someday required by a different employer. And that's why people hate them so.

But, okay, what type of person has no difficulty exchanging one hat for another on the rack whenever the job requires it? Well, actors seem to have the uncanny ability to flip-flop all over the personality spectrum. But, we know that about actors. They are expected to be Han Solo for a few months, then Indiana Jones the next, then Rusty Sabich, and so on. Who cares if they change their spots?

(of course, the scary thing is that we revere these actors as though they were gods or something. We plan our weeknights around what TV show is on and then dress up on the weekends like the magazines tell us our favorite star dresses up; we cry like babies when Julia Roberts dies, or when Shoeless Joe says, "If you build it," and then, casting a glance at Ray's father out on the field, "he will come." And we forgive them for all of their trespasses: wife-beating, adultery, even homicide, not to mention the river-esque flow of drugs, drugs, drugs. Rehab and Betty Ford and shooting cars and stabbing parents and killing children, and, in the midst of chaos and mutiny, we sit at tea and argue the qualities of the Liz-Taylor husband we liked the most. Hmmmmmmmmm. Maybe we deserve the lawyers we get...)

Anyway, where was I? Oh, yes, the poor lawyer who has to wear so many hats.

I guess the whole hypocrisy of practicing law arrives at its legitimacy because it is all written down in such big books. Every word of every appellate decision in the Country is recorded in at least one "Reporter," and almost always more than one. Each state has a Reporter, and the Nation is broken down into regions, which have Reporters. Then there are the Federal Appellate Reporters, the Federal Supplements and, of course, the Supreme Court Reporter. So many reporters, so many words and case citations and decisions and opinions and blah, blah, blah. You'd be normal if you thought to yourself, "Hey, with all those reporters out there, how do the companies that publish them know what the others have written? How do the various competitors in the law publishing business keep things standard enough so that the lawyers will be able to find what it is they're looking for?"

Your question is fatally flawed.

There are no "competitors."

There is only West. West Publishing Company. West. That's it.

All of everything done in the law, when it comes to writing it down, West does it. Okay, there are one or two wannabe's, but, like the Red Sox, there is only one West. And, I know you'll find this fact amazing and unbelievable: West is run by lawyers. When West writes it, it is THE LAW. Give a judge a copy of a case from one of those "other" publishing companies, and he or she will scoff, or frown, furrow the brow a little, maybe even a tilt of the head and a scratch, and say, "Do you have the *West* of this case?" What I'm telling you is that the entire legal system, "not perfect but the best system in the world," stands on the essentially unchallenged, and unchallengeable, shoulders of one company. Add that to the fact that nine people have the final say so for everything we can and cannot do, and you've got yourself a first class monopoly, just like Ma Bell and Microsoft.

So, pick up a Supreme Court Reporter from a hundred years or so ago, and start reading. You will be amazed at the clarity and economy of language you will find in these opinions. And, logic. Logic that follows yours, so closely that you find the question raised in your mind by one sentence answered by the next. You won't find that in the British texts, which preceded our own by centuries, a positive holdover from the Revolution, I suppose.

In the British texts, one has the feeling the writer is paid by the word:

"It is essentially clear and unequivocated, and unchallenged by any convincing or plausible or otherwise acceptable argument made by either the Barrister or his assigns, that Master Bates of Lancashire Proper, whilst journeying in a direction agreed by the parties to be west towards Suffolkshire late in the forenoon of the day in question, Fifth March, in the Year of Our Lord Seventeen and Naught Five, was approached from the opposite direction by Master Thornton, of Suffolkshire. Neither one willing to give leave to the other, or perhaps able, given the nature and condition of the thoroughfare on the day in question, Fifth March, in the Year of Our Lord, Seventeen and Naught Five, and the result of that juxtaposition being unclear, our decision to day must indeed rest on the well-settled legal tenet that the west-proceeding buggy, if opined to be the larger of the twain and not containing a lady...." You get the point. I mean, they had little else to do, so why not spend an hour to say what we say in a few moments in the modern world?

And here's the heck of it: Shakespeare was poking fun at lawyers when he thwarted Shylock's attempt to take a pound of flesh. He wasn't trying to help them! Yet lawyers throughout history have seized on the Merchant's loophole. You see, the Merchant's contract was vague, and therefore subject to sufficient alternative interpretations that it ended up having no teeth. A savvy lawyer would have written something like this:

"...party of the first part shall be awarded damages in the amount of approximately one (1) pound of flesh from the body of party of the second part. Said one (1) pound to be determined following examination by a trained professional in the medical field and shall be understood to include any and all substances directly proximate to or a part of said pound of flesh, including but not limited to blood (including all corpuscles and any other liquid contained therein), venous and arterial tissue, muscle, fat, hair, and all layers of the dermis." A complete or at least nearly complete dissertation of all that would allow a court to determine *in futuro* that the loser actually agreed to be maimed. No appeals court could overturn that, not without finding that the agreement "shocked the conscience of the court."

Writing is at the very core of what lawyers do; all those funny-sounding words and matter-of-fact, legally-supported threats you get in the mail would be nothing without the "craft" of legal writing.

When a literary scholar sets about to deconstruct a piece of literature, he or she is bent upon determining the writer's motivation, state of mind, and intent. Knowing full well that the writer chose each and every word very carefully so as to evoke a desired response in the reader, the deconstructionist uses those words as a kind of road map, or, better yet, a treasure map. The deconstructionist should be able, having spent some time within the writer's work, to predict a certain outcome based upon a recurring pattern unique to that writer. Agatha Christie is regarded as perhaps the foremost playwright of mystery the world has ever known. Anyone who has enjoyed her writing knows full well that, at some point within the play, several people will be gathered in the library or study of a grand old estate, a man will be dead, and a local highly-intuitive inspector will reconstruct the murder. And, of course, all present will be suspect.

William Goldman is one of my favorite writers. Beginning his career as a novelist, Goldman moved quickly up the Hollywood ranks as one of that industry's best known screenwriters.

I always enjoyed Goldman's conversational style, and I guess I picked that up from him, to a degree. I have consciously utilized some of his techniques in previous works, and even in this book. Goldman—when it is appropriate—will use long dashes instead of commas to separate related but not integral thoughts within a single sentence. But my favorite of all of Goldman's techniques is best used sparingly, and it comes after a paragraph of some length, usually containing a string of setup phrases, clauses, and fragments, and is like the last hammer swing that drives the nail home.

A short line paragraph.

Sometimes followed by another.

And occasionally finishing the thought process with yet another.

You say, "Wendell, what the heck are you doing with all this literary yap?" (*Asking your question for you is another one of my techniques, a holdover from when I was a newspaper columnist in North Carolina, sorry*). What I'm trying to show you is that in all writing the author is attempting to use his words to do something to the reader, whether it's to provoke, convince, clarify or convey, describe, detail, decry or dismay (*very sorry*).

In the legal world, the author is almost always trying to convince the reader of something (*or, in the case of a threatening letter from a lawyer, trying to separate you from your money*). Sure, it looks like a basic recitation of the law and the facts of the case written up and provided to a client or another lawyer or a court for informational purposes. But it's an argument, and the skilled legal writer will craft the document such that it paints his or her side of the case in the best light.

If it is an appellate court's opinion, the court realizes that its words will be forever encapsulated in a Reporter somewhere, like "Jamie, 1956" in a replacement section of a concrete walkway of a suburban home. And just like that replacement segment, the opinion has to "fit." It has to provide the proper footing to the next section, without requiring the one who's walking to go too far out of his way to get to the next section. In the Law, that piece of concrete is something called "Precedent."

To understand why we've gotten so off-track as a society, you have to embrace the process of Precedent. In the Law, Precedent is the act of using another established legal tenet (preferably in your jurisdiction but not always necessary) to bolster your argument and provide a judge with the legal ability to rule in your favor. The entire concept of precedent—building one's case upon the continually affirmed legal history of the law in a given jurisdiction—is the heart of the law. A lawyer needn't rely upon his or her own theory or strategy or ideas all that often. Most of the law that happens everyday has already been done so much that the outcome of most cases is a given. Okay, we read and hear about unique and challenging cases now and then, the kind of cases that so challenge the accepted tenets of the law that an appeals court has to hear them, to apply constitutional mandates from eons ago to a very modern day dispute (dealt with quite nicely in a future chapter in this book). But the bulk of the law that pays the bills of the lawyers is carved in stone. The "black letter law" of the variety of areas of the law—torts, contracts, and most especially criminal—is so predictable now that many civil lawyers can offer to take a good case without any fee unless the client wins. Their "free initial consultation" allows the law firm to winnow out the questionable cases so that all they have are almost sure winners, cases that will almost always settle out of court.

And that winnowing process has so much to do with precedent. A student or practitioner of the law knows full well the usual outcome of a simple tort case because the generations of appellate decisions have affirmed and re-affirmed the legal remedy. We know, for instance, that if you own or possess an item deemed to be an "inherently dangerous instrumentality" and it causes harm to another, you are liable. Called "Strict Liability" because there are no steps you can take to sufficiently insulate you from culpability, the list includes several items based upon your jurisdiction. The example is often used of a pet lion. A lion is deemed to be a dangerous instrumentality based upon its capacity for harm versus its ability to be controlled 100 per cent of the time. Even circus performers who have owned and trained a cat for years have been killed by that lion. So, no matter if you build a huge enclosure with massive bars and walls and locks and bury it in the ground so that your lion has almost no chance of escaping, if he does and hurts somebody, you are liable. There is no defense available to you as the owner of this dangerous instrumentality.

Gerry Spence used the "inherently dangerous instrumentality" argument when he handled the well-known Karen Silkwood case. In that case, Silkwood worked for Kerr-McGee, a uranium processing plant for the electric industry, and she became contaminated with uranium, which caused her cancer. Spence argued that uranium was so dangerous an instrumentality that if it leaked or "got away", the company had to pay. The company's lawyers argued that Silkwood, a union organizer, allowed herself to be contaminated in order to gain support for the union from the workforce. Silkwood mysteriously died in a one-car accident before her case could really see the light of day,[10] but the notion that uranium could be an inher-

---

10 Spence won a $10.5 million award for Silkwood's children, but an appeals court "remit-titured" (discounted) the award, basically saying that the children wouldn't know what to do with so much money.

ently dangerous instrumentality led to significant cut-backs in nuclear power.

Interestingly enough, however, the Supreme Court has decided that a firearm is not an inherently dangerous instrumentality. Unlike a lion or uranium, the Court says, a firearm's design is to *cause* harm, and is therefore exempt from strict liability. The modern day Supreme Court held this way in order to stem an endless tide of lawsuits against gun manufacturers, owners, and, most decidedly, police officers, whose guns are sometimes used to cause harm.

Okay, okay, enough about Strict Liability. The example here is used so that you understand that there are areas, many areas, of the law in which the same outcome has been arrived at so often that a lawyer practically knows how his or her set of facts will stack up at the get-go.

What I'd like you to understand here is the notion that another, or others, is responsible for a certain outcome. Cases through the years allow a lawyer to hang his or her hat securely upon them, without rendering a moral judgment on the case at hand, and, most importantly, without having to take a stand. (Later on, we'll talk about how judges tenuously attach their hidden agenda to shaky precedent, and how that process has really perverted the Law.)

For instance, a client wheels into a lawyer's office and declares that she has slipped and fallen in a local grocery store, resulting in injuries. After only a few questions, the lawyer reveals enough information to make a preliminary decision that this case is cut and dried. Although "slip and fall" type injuries are not strict liability cases, most grocery stores will settle these cases without much of a fight. Why? Because the cost of fighting the cases (in terms of Legal Fees and costs) is almost always higher than the average settlement cost. Add to that the possibility of losing at trial, and the cost of the litigation—in both monetary and bad publicity terms—can be astronomical.

So, why is that a bad thing, you may ask. Because of what the lawyer doesn't ask, and doesn't want to know. The client, usually an overweight, out of shape, middle-aged woman (those are the statistics, mind you) has "slipped and fallen" before. In fact, she seems to make a habit of slipping and falling in grocery stores. Truth is she makes a *living* at it! But, unless somebody does some very good investigation, and assuming a court will not allow the prior act evidence to be admitted, nobody will ever know about it.

Okay, I can see I've got to break that down. You would think, in your reasonable, logical way of thinking, that, number one, the lawyer for the grocery store (really the lawyer for the *insurance company* for the grocery store) would do the leg work to find out about the woman's past activities in the produce section, and, number two, that the court would want to know about it. Well, two things are working against our logic there. The first is the privacy of settlements, and the second is the Hearsay Rule.

You may have heard that settlement agreements are often sealed, and that a party may not divulge the contents of a settlement agreement to anybody, or he will lose his settlement. Companies do this so that the world doesn't find out how much it paid to a litigant to prevent the matter from going to court, lest it encourage others from seeking their fortune in such a manner. A settlement usually relieves an at-fault party from actually admitting that fault, in the legal sense (and especially in the courtroom or, worse yet, in one of those Reporters mentioned above). Settlements provide a tidy method of "making a problem go away," and, as we said above, save Defendants a ton of money. In our case above, if no past litigant is allowed to divulge the details of the settlement arrangement, then it is as if it doesn't even exist. That's where number two comes in.

The Hearsay Rule. The Hearsay Rule is simple, as long as you remember one acronym: OPTMA. *Offered to Prove The Matter Asserted.* If proffered evidence is being offered to prove the matter therein asserted (sorry) then it is hearsay and is excluded from testimony "He told me he was going to go over and kill the neighbor," if offered to prove that he killed the neighbor, is hearsay and cannot be admitted.

But guess what?

There are exceptions to the Hearsay Rule. Tons of 'em.

For instance, let' s say in our brief example above that the man who went over to kill the neighbor ends up dead himself, and our neighbor's defense to the killing is self-defense. Now, the speaker in our statement, in order to show the dead man's "state of mind" may step up on the witness stand and say his statement, and it lends itself to credible evidence that the neighbor may have killed him in self-defense. Again, it is not being offered to *prove* self-defense, only the dead person's *state of mind*, and that is an exception to the Hearsay rule.

I had a judge in Chattanooga, Tennessee tell me that the hearsay rule only applied to what people said. He thought since I was a new lawyer he'd educate me, and told me, "now counselor, don't use phrases like 'he said' or 'she said,' 'cause that's hearsay." When I told him I was not using the evidence to prove the matter asserted, only to show the speaker's state of mind, he said that didn't matter. I pulled out my little green evidence book and showed him that he was wrong; later, he summarily dismissed my case. Turns out he was educating me after all: Never argue with the Judge.

Now, the Hearsay rule prevents evidence of previous acts from being admitted. Let's assume that the three previous slip-

and-falls of our grocery store "victim" were not settled but actually went to court. Even though she's slipped and fallen three times before in local grocery stores, that evidence cannot be admitted and she cannot be challenged on that point because the Hearsay rule says that just because somebody has done something before doesn't mean they will do or have done it again.

Unless.

Unless one can establish a "pattern of behavior." A guy has been arrested and convicted six times of holding up convenience stores wearing a blue trench coat and holding a sawed-off shotgun. It is his *modus opperendi* or his "M.O." The evidence shows that this time the convenience store was held up by a man wearing a blue trench coat and brandishing a sawed-off shotgun. That's pattern evidence and likely to be admitted at trial (of course, this case doesn't go to trial, but is plea-bargained out, but for now, let's leave the real world out of it; lawyers always do).

So, Wendell, you ask, what about our lady with the bad balance? Uh-uh-uh...you forgot about our number one. Really, even though we said let's pretend she went to trial three times before, actually she didn't. There's no trial, so there's no record, so there's no evidence. So, there's no pattern. Besides, a court could just as easily say that this woman is accident-prone and grocery stores should be more careful.

The point is that the lawyer has so many things to hang his hat on, that he doesn't even have to worry about making a decision other than whether to take the case and accept the large legal fee that accompanies it. Do that day in and day out and you will soon find it unnecessary to make any kind of thoughtful decision at all. There will be no right or wrong, only admissible and inadmissible. There is no should or shouldn't, only collectible or uncollectible. There is no could or couldn't, only winning or losing. The law doesn't want lawyers to make the kind of judgments reserved for the courts. "Bring all the cases," the Law cries out, "and we will render judgment."

With moral judgment and irrelevant truth set aside, the lawyer need only focus in on the important stuff: Getting a fee and making an argument.

But there are people in every community, every walk of life, who have disputes, real grievances, mind you, that will never see the inside of a courtroom. People injured by others, people who've had property taken, people who've lost jobs. They will never see justice because there is no large fee, or there is too much capacity for failure, or there is too much thoughtfulness required to get to the jury. Our lawyer above, with time to only ask a few "pertinent" questions, will never take the case of a single pregnant mom who got fired from Burger King because she couldn't lift a large ice bin. Or the lady who bought a lemon used car who got the runaround from the shady dealer. Or the guy who had his antique tools stolen from a despicable Realtor using a lock-box key.

There used to be a cadre of lawyers, caring individuals trying to make the world a better place, who took the time to represent poor clients with less than earth shattering cases. In fact, the various bar associations encourage *pro bono*[11] work. And sure, there's the local Legal Aid Society, but their workload makes the probation officer look like a member of the UAW. But, as you may imagine, these lawyers are working men and women, devoid of the free time required to do the networking and make the connections at the local watering hole, or on the golf course. Armed with only shaky precedent and sometimes

---

11 Shortened form of *Pro Bono Publico* or "for the public good". In the Law, if means providing legal services free of charge.

even shakier clients, they stand in front of a judge in an off-the-rack suit and make an argument. The old-fashioned way.

By and large, these lawyers are gone. Some fresh law school grads take these kinds of jobs (as well as in the Prosecutor's office and, particularly the Public Defender) in order to get their feet wet and make a little bit of money. I did. Quickly swamped by an office filled with files, these bright-eyed men and women constantly seek the exit door. Like newly minted flight instructors only building up time until they land that plum airline job, public interest lawyers, for the most part, are only paying their dues. To the ones who stick it out and make a career of vindicating the rights of the downtrodden, I say "good for you," because the others will always think less of you.

But most lawyers use the time in public service learning how to change hats. And it isn't long before they graduate to the place where they'll spend their days crafting half-truths and erecting walls around disclosure, because the alternative would most likely lead to a speedy resolution and less money.

And what self-respecting distinguished member of the bar wants that?

31 Flavors of Law

One of the reasons the law has gotten so out of hand is what I like to call the "31 Flavors" problem. You see, when I was a very young boy growing up in New England, there were, at most, three flavors of ice cream at any given ice cream shop. For that matter, there were very few ice cream shops at all. And, in reality, there were usually only two flavors. And, in a good number of shops, one.

Vanilla.

Chocolate.

Strawberry.

If you were a person who liked vanilla ice cream, well, that said a lot about whom you were. You liked things orderly, predictable. You bought a conservative white automobile and changed the oil every three-thousand miles and drove the speed limit and stopped at every stop sign and kept it full of gas and you knew what your life was going to be like tomorrow and the next day and each and every day after that. And vanilla was so available. It's still the most popular flavor of ice cream in the world, why mess with it?

If you were chocolate, you were much different from vanilla, you liked a little zing to your day. You might have a green car or a blue car or maybe even two-toned. You weren't really frightened that the Ruskies might just be knocking at the door, and you stayed up late to watch movies where you might see a man and woman in bed together. Essentially, however, you liked the orderly, the routine. Mostly, though, you were simply not vanilla. Sure, you had ideals, and yes, you had beliefs that you had kept forever. But they were the opposite of vanilla.

If you were strawberry, you were the zany fools who wore sunglasses in the nighttime and drove red convertible sports cars and you were the first to grow your hair long or wear hot pants and you didn't always believe everything you read in a newspaper or saw on television and you tried to understand your parents but, after all, they were soooooooo very vanilla.

So you have two, or at the most, three flavors. That was enough. Vanilla and Chocolate (forget Strawberry for right now).

Kennedy was Vanilla, Kruschev was Chocolate.

Patton was Vanilla, Hitler was Chocolate.

Pat Boone was quite Vanilla, the Beatles were highly Chocolate.

The American Army was Vanilla; Charlie was Chocolate.

We knew what to expect, and we expected so little. The United States was superior and philosophically correct and all those other "heathen" countries needed "civilizing." We were the Peace Corps and UNICEF and Missionaries and we just knew what was right and what was wrong.

Sam Sheppard killed his wife, we were pretty sure of that. Immigrant thieves stole the Lindbergh baby, we knew that. Oswald killed Kennedy because he made Castro look bad. We definitely knew that. Ed Sullivan was on Sunday night right after the *Wonderful World of Color*, our drinking water was safe, and the only way to deal with those yellow japs was to eradicate their race from the face of the Earth, and why in the world do those Negroes want to go to school or ride the bus or sit at the same lunch counter as we whites? There were three television networks and they all had the news on at six p.m. And they spoke the gospel truth.

Vanilla and Chocolate. Black and White.

And that's how we wanted our law. Guilty or Not Guilty. Liable or Not Liable. Truth or Lie. But there's a problem with black and white law that is the same as the problem with three television networks that is the same as two flavors of ice cream: There Ain't No Money In That.

Take for instance that guy or woman who said, "Hey, what about a berry flavor of ice cream? What about Strawberry, for instance?" What that person did was exhibit a natural human reaction to a vanilla and chocolate world. And with that one "what if?" he or she opened the gate through which Mr. Baskin and Mr. Robbins were happy to pass. By saying, "What about a different flavor of ice cream for each day of the month?" Baskin Robbins blew our minds.[12] It is the gastrointestinal equal to Robert Kennedy saying, "…I dream of things that never were and ask, 'why not?'"

So, along comes a young bulldog of a defense attorney named Frances Lee Bailey who, I'd like to think innocently, takes a look at an old murder case and a new machine called a "Polygraph," and a very new method of crime interpretation called "forensics," and applies the Baskin-Robbins test to it all.

Dr. Sam Sheppard was, by all accounts, a very good doctor and a talented surgeon. He appeared to have a perfect home life, a good wife, plenty of money, friends, influence. When those friends found out that his dear wife had been bludgeoned to death in her own bedroom, many of them searched for strawberry. Despite all evidence to the contrary, many of Sam Sheppard's friends chose to believe his account of encountering an

---

12. A nod must be given to Mr. Howard Johnson, who served 28 flavors of ice cream in his restaurants well before Baskin/Robbins.

oversized blurry intruder who, devoid of motive, brutally killed Mrs. Sheppard while fleeing from the drunken, stupefied, half-awake good doctor. All they needed was a shred or two of corroborating evidence to completely discard the obvious truth: that Sam Sheppard, for one reason or another (maybe even for a third), lost control of himself and allowed an evening's worth of alcohol its head and viciously killed his wife.

Ten years after a contemporary jury of his peers—in a community rife with his political and social allies—rendered him guilty, F. Lee Bailey gave Dr. Sheppard's friends their strawberry. Bailey filed a *habeus corpus*[13] petition to allow him to present the evidence in a new light, given the advances (at the time) in forensics and polygraph. He vigorously argued minute points of the law and of the facts, particularly the facts, sufficient to release Sheppard and get him a new trial, at which he was acquitted.

Bailey had an expert testify that the blood splatters on the Sheppard's bedroom wall could only have come from somebody wielding a blunt instrument with his or her left hand. Sheppard, as it was testified to, was right handed. That was stunning evidence, to most. When I read Bailey's account of that evidence, I immediately thought of Reggie Smith, the athletic, switch-hitting center fielder for the Boston Red Sox.

Bailey also shone the light on Sheppard's upper back injury, illustrating that another must have been in the house since Sheppard could not have administered the blow to himself. Yet, later in the testimony, Sheppard indicated that he had jumped from the second story porch to the beach below in hasty chase of the blurry intruder, and even testified that he landed on his

---

13 Literally to "produce the body." In the law, it means a person may defend himself from unlawful detention or an unlawful or evidentially unsupported conviction.

back! Somehow, the correlation between that fall and the injury escaped the new-trial jury.

Bailey executed his smoke and mirrors show with the expertise of a seasoned magician, all with only one simple goal in mind: Reasonable Doubt. Bailey convinced the judge to issue an instruction to the effect that "beyond a reasonable doubt is not the same as 'beyond the shadow of a doubt,'" which, I would agree, is proper. But it was quite new indeed to clutter the jury's mind with such hair-splitting jargon, and Reasonable Doubt became, at that moment, the prize of the entire criminal defense bar. In reality, it became what it still is today: A Way Out. Juries bent on acquittal will find some microscopic shred of evidence that leans away from guilt and hang their "reasonable doubt" hat upon it. In their minds, it is simply vanilla with a red hue. In the hearts of crime victims and their loved ones, it is the abomination of Rocky Road.

But why are juries bent upon acquittal anyway? It's a good question and, I believe has its roots in two very different aspects of American Life.

First, there are the first ten amendments to the Constitution, collectively referred to as the "Bill of Rights." The Bill of Rights was written by, primarily, Thomas Jefferson and James Madison via a compromise in order to get the Constitution ratified. Without the Bill of Rights, too many colonists who fought for freedom from anarchy would have found little of substance in the Constitution for any but the wealthy slave-owners who had drafted it, and likely would have mounted yet another revolt. Remember, the country was resting on very shaky ground at this time. So, the powers that be withdrew their quills and set about to articulate all the ills of King George's monarchy, and to forever prevent that kind of tyranny in the union. If you wanted to say something, even something against the government (who would want to then?), why just go ahead. Want to worship Buddha? (uh, like who, man?) Go ahead. And, in case the new government just happens to try to brutalize you like old George had, well, you have the guns, you can revolt!

You could no longer be dragged into a Star Chamber and be forced to tell it what wrong you have done; that's what the famous Fifth Amendment is really all about. And, when you were charged with a crime, you had the right to be represented by an upstanding member of the bar who had studied the law and its intricacies, so you wouldn't be railroaded into prison, or, worse, to the gallows.

The historical rationale behind the Bill of Rights, and the intentions of the framers, while noble and forthright, could never have anticipated a world of motorcars or television, let alone aircraft, computers or professional sports. In an effort to keep the United States solidified at any cost, the interpreters of the Constitution have used everything from gymnastics to a Saladmaster, and the results are anything but aesthetically pleasing or palatable. And the lawyers and judges and justices say, "There it is, folks, pistachio almond mocha cherry fudge ripple banana! What do you mean you don't like it? Why, the world is a complex place, one the framers of the Constitution could not fathom. It is, therefore, up to us to fathom it for them. So here's a result that should please everyone." The truth, the elephant in the living room, is that the results often please no one except the lawyers who are so proud of themselves for covering all the bases and using all the "WHEREFORE"s in all the right places.

Which brings me to the second, distant, reason.

With all the multitude of flavors and all the hundreds of television channels and the scores of cereal on the cereal aisle and the five-hundred suits to choose from and the gazillions of shoes and cars and sunglasses and purses and the sixty different entrees at Mr. Chang's, people like the distinguished (not my characterization) Mr. Bailey have decided that there should be something other than Guilty and Not Guilty. So, now we have "*Nolo Contendre.*" Wow. Latin for "No Contest," Nolo Contendre means the accused is not admitting guilt, but does not wish to contest the charges. A product of the late twentieth century necessity for the plea bargain, "Nolo" allowed a person to take a plea without admitting guilt. It is sad commentary on a civilized country indeed that innocent people wrongly charged with a crime are unable to arm themselves with the truth in order to defeat misfiled charges, and must resort to some kind of punishment—the lesser of two evils—in order to avoid certain conviction, and a much more severe penalty should the matter proceed to trial. "The Truth," the Bible says, "shall set you free." It does not go on to say that such is the case in this "One Nation Under God."

The problem with Nolo is the same problem with Strawberry: It paved the way for all kinds of mutant pleas. But, more than this it allowed the people the same mealy-mouthed ability to shed responsibility as do their lawyers.

Not Guilty By Reason of Insanity.

Not Guilty By Reason of Temporary Insanity.

Not Guilty By Reason of Self Defense.

Guilty But Mentally Impaired.

Not Guilty By Reason of Inability To Comprehend His or Her Actions At The Time Of The Crime.

And Non Compos Mentes, or not mentally competent to stand trial.

These are but a few of the creations that lawyers and judges and justices have assembled, with the help of the Bill of Rights, to accommodate the legion of twentieth-century social deviants. A constitution that bends and stretches in penance for the sins of its drafters and subsequent practitioners is not a constitution at all. A constitution that continually re-defines its borders in an effort to contain all contains none. A justice system that morphs itself at the whim of political pressure, necessarily sacrifices justice itself, leaving it in the dust with Truth its only companion.

In actuality, what really happened in the fifties, sixties and seventies is that all Hell broke loose. Literally. A once God-fearing country removed God from His rightful place at the head of this potentially great nation, and, perhaps inadvertently, invited Satan to take God's place.

It's that simple.

Once God was gone, all that He stands for went with it. Morality, Truth, Honesty, Kindness, Patience, Forgiveness, Love. And, to paraphrase a popular saying, a country that stands for nothing will fall for anything.

But you say, "Wendell, doesn't God embrace all? Red and yellow black and white and all that? Where does your whole Vanilla and Chocolate argument stand up under that scrutiny?"

Good question. Again, however, we have somebody trying to attach supernatural law to natural people, saying there is right and wrong in the eyes of God, there must be right and wrong people. But God is not so judgmental. He loves us for who we are, knowing full well that we are going to disappoint Him, and that we are not like the Sun or the Moon or the wind or water, we don't follow the laws He established for the things of the world that are not His greatest creation. It comes down to the old adage, "Hate the sin, love the sinner." Once we embrace the fact that it is not we who are "bad," but the work of Satan in our hearts that leads, and has led, us astray, we can more easily accept the Truths that God has established for us.

I think the Civil Rights movement in America also participated in the precipitation of the layering of society. Forever seeing the world in terms of white and black, good and evil, right and wrong, extremes, we whites were forced to see that those we believed to be different, inferior, second-class, an abomination, were, in fact, our brothers and sisters in Christ. That acceptance, which has never and will never be complete, created a phenomenon called "Cognitive Dissonance," a term psychologists use to define that moment when we are faced with evidence which clearly refutes our deepest held beliefs, or something like that. Once that structure is chipped at, our notions of absolutes begins to waver and we begin to question all that we hold dear, pausing briefly for a moment or two of denial, and taking a trip down a slippery slope until nothing is absolute, nothing is vanilla, nothing is chocolate, and any old morsel of contrary evidence becomes "reasonable doubt."

And, every time that happens, every time Sam Sheppard or O.J. Simpson—people our gut tells us to be culpable of unspeakable atrocities—every time they walk the earth freely, it only serves to solidify the insecurities and instabilities that plague us into believing that nothing is absolute anymore.

And that is when Satan dances with glee. Satan's agenda is to confound, complicate, confuse and, ultimately, divide. God wants us ALL in His kingdom; Satan wants none of us in God's kingdom.

It's Vanilla and Chocolate and the choice is really simple. 31 flavors of law, two roads, one People.

Unfortunately for the People, there will always be more law. Its cells continue to divide and sub-divide creating an all-encompassing array of regulation and restriction that has all but destroyed the freedom-filled existence envisioned by the Founding Fathers. And it's not as though an old law is retired when a new law is enacted. More law equals more lawyers, and more lawyers equal more law. Thomas Jefferson charged the People to be "eternally vigilant" in our Republic, to maintain a check on a centralized federal government whose nature is to become more centralized, stronger and more oppressive.

Perhaps our most significant blunder is that We the People delegated that duty to our lawyers.

Waffling Away Accountability

Lawyers are often called upon to maintain two entirely polar positions simultaneously. For instance, a lawyer representing a bank in a simple foreclosure suit against a mortgagor may also be defending a mortgagor sued in foreclosure against a different bank. In the morning, our lawyer argues,

"Judge, these defendants have had four months to bring this mortgage up to date, and they just will not comply. My client has shown a great deal of leniency, but can no longer tolerate this delinquency. The law is clear in this area."

In the afternoon, in front of the same judge but this time arguing for a family faced with foreclosure and eviction (by a different lender, mind you), says, "Judge, my clients have tried to bring this account up to date, but the lender simply won't budge, and the interest and late fees are usurious and the lender is engaging in illegal behavior in violation of the Federal Fair Debt Collection Act….blah blah blah…. The Law is clear in this area."

You might think that such a situation might be illegal or unethical, based on your lay understanding of the difference between right and wrong. I mean, when a person says one thing to one person, and, on the same topic a different thing to another person, we say he is "talking out of both sides of his mouth," or, "giving lip service" to one or both of his listeners. But, a lawyer who exhibits this same conduct is "being a strong and unbiased advocate." Not only is such conduct not censured or forbidden by the organized bar, it is *encouraged!* In fact, one set of bar rules says, "The lawyer should not attempt to inject his or her personal bias regarding the success or failure of a certain legal theory over another, or make judgments concerning the success or failure of a law suit; he or she should tender advice only, based upon a clear interpretation of the law."

A lawyer may tell you that his simultaneous—and vigorous—loyalty to opposing theories or arguments actually broadens his scope and understanding of the legal issue involved. She may say that by entertaining all sides in an issue she is allowed to fully appreciate the complexity of the situation, and give all potential outcomes their opportunity to prevail. The problem with this logic, or absence of it, is that it probes only the lifeless, mind-centered words, and completely ignores the nagging voice of conscience that already knows the truth long before the learned counselor tried to confuse it with her "superior" mind. And, what that lawyer will not tell you is the real truth: a paying client is a paying client. A good lawyer will adopt the requisite position depending upon who is buttering the bread.

But, you see the problem here isn't one of truth or justice or even a conflict of interest. The problem is that of *accountability*. Lawyers are expected to advocate for the client, not themselves. We assume that the lawyer is unbiased and unattached and only engages in discovery and cross-examination on behalf of the client. We expect him or her to change his or her tune for each client, but require consistency and integrity when he or she, say, enters public office. But, they can't change. They can't change because they've spent a career lying to themselves, so much so that, if they ever did hold to a dogma or a creed or even a strong, heartfelt conviction, the law has long since kicked it clean out of them. Which is why, when all the evidence points to the fact that the president of the United States has been serviced orally by a White House intern, he retreats into the dark labyrinth that is the Law, and mounts his best defense: oral sex isn't sex, not really.

(And what do people say? "GREAT!" "Terrific!" Married men from Austin to Boston sigh a collective "whew," and wipe their brows and grab their wives by the arm and point their fingers at the T.V. and say, "See, honey, I told you I never cheated on you!" Married women stop gnawing at their lower lip and can spend a few moments less in the confessional. But that's not really what this book is about…or is it?)

Like it or not, we Americans look to our leadership for guidance. Sure, we ridicule and dismiss them as though we were rebellious adolescents and they our worthless parents. But the worthless parent is an example nonetheless. The worthless parent lacking leadership still provides guidance! More than one therapist will tell you that parents, more than any other group or individual, influence their children's progress into adulthood. Permissive parents often raise children who are uncomfortable with boundaries and authority, while overly-strict parents see their offspring explode into society with vengeance.

My own parents, for instance, did not walk around the house in their underwear. It occurred to me that to do so was wrong, what with "little children" teeming about. But, when I was in high school, I was over a friend's house, and his parents walked about freely in their underwear, and they were some large people, let me tell you. I thought, "hey man, that's cool." I went home and told my Mom, "Ted's parents walk around in their underwear, why can't I?"

Of course, based upon that evidence I cannot now overstate the influence upon us by our elected officials or teachers or coaches. But these peripheral authority figures do provide guidance, set an example of how we should live our lives, how we can live our lives. Now a large part of this country is saying, "Bill gets oral sex from a woman who's not his wife and he says he did nothing wrong, why can't I?"

The answer is, of course, when you can convince yourself of such an absurd conclusion, when you believe the truth of that entirely unbelievable lie, then, and only then, can you follow President Clinton's lead with a clear conscience.

Which, of course, is what lawyers do, day in and day out, until there is no right or wrong, only a temporary indignant, unwavering stance. If you read only one paragraph of this book, let it be this one, for it is the focal point of the entire argument. Just as former President Clinton rubber-stamped casual, extra-marital sexual relations, so do lawyers rubber-stamp the accepted ability to look and see only that which we want to see. And it would end there, really, if it weren't for one natural law: Lawyers would get out of the way of a speeding locomotive.

Aha! You see? Even if a lawyer had convinced himself that the train would, clearly and without even the shadow of a doubt (your Honor), pass through him and leave him uninjured, when faced with the physical reality would be forced to admit the flaw in his argument (or join his colleagues in what I pray is a special Hell). Oh, sure, he could probably find a way to cast doubts on your belief that there is, indeed, a pachyderm perched on you porch (unless the opposite argument held more money, er, promise). But tied to the track with a rag in his mouth upon a cushion of sinister piano music, he'd have to fess up.

And at that point, right when the whites of his eyes are obliterated by pupils the size of walnuts, he would see clearly east and west, up and down, right and wrong, truth and lie.

Life would reassume its certain polarity, and there would be no more grey.

Except for the elephant in the living room, that he used to simply vacuum around.

So, why do it? Why spend so much time and energy sorting through the wreckage of the injured victim, or the usually good guy who loses his temper and takes a Louisville Slugger to the guy who cut him off, or the contractor who thinned out the cement mix, or whoever finds himself in need of a lawyer?

Well, we're back at the same place we were a few minutes ago...money. Only money, the lure of it, the power of gold, brings out the true insanity that is the practice of the law. For a few, there is tons of money. Ooodles. Sacks. Hand over fist. Whoever coined the phrase, "license to steal," was right. In no other arena is the unearned income potential so great.

By the way, it doesn't really matter where you get your legal education, mind you; you get the same education at a state school as you do at Harvard or Stanford, it just costs more there and the plum firms look there first. Ohhhhh..you're surprised, eh? You shouldn't be; by now you should be able to discern that the difference between Harvard and the University of Massachusetts is but a short subway ride and tens upon tens of thousands of dollars.

So, a few thousand dollars at the University of Wherever and Wham! You've got yourself a law degree. A few thousand more to one of the Bar Test Prep companies, and you've got yourself a passing grade on the Bar Exam. These companies take your money, a few thousand or so, and send you a kit and some videos, or perhaps even allows you to attend some classes. And you have all you need to get by any of the state's bar exams, and the all mysterious Multi-State Bar Exam

Wait a minute, Wendell...what about Law School? Doesn't it teach you about the Bar Exam? Don't they have some courses in how to pass the Bar Exam? I mean, after all, you spent all the money to get a FIRST CLASS LEGAL EDUCATION, at least they could tell you the information contained on the BAR EXAM, couldn't they??

Um, well, er, nope. Not a shred of information about the exam itself. Sure, there're Torts and Contracts and Criminal Law and Procedure and all the crap...stuff that's *on* the exam. But nothing about how to answer the convoluted questions in each of those areas agonizingly posed by a sadistic team of bar examiners. Which is where the Bar Exam Test Preparation Companies come in. (*By the way, guess who owns the largest and most successful prep course? West Publishing Company! No Kidding!*)

After pounding your head against the law for three years in law school, staying up all night and cramming and debating and making end-arounds in the law library so that only you get your hands on the all important text or reporter or whatever that everybody needs to complete an assignment...after all of that, there are several weeks in bar preparation, in which you learn how to pass the bar exam.

Oh, my, I am wandering about in this chapter, am I not? Well, it just gets my blood boiling, is all. I'm not really sure, but I think it's at least possible that many of the lecturers for the bar prep companies never represented a client. Ironically, though, they epitomize the practice of law: Go Where The Money Is. In his case, law students who must pass the bar exam represent the most target-rich environment.

Okay, back to the premise of this chapter.

Perhaps the most glaring example of the advocate multi-personality doctrine is the Prosecutor About Face. After years in the District Attorney's office (sometimes called the "Prosecutor" or the "State's Attorney"), making the state's case against criminals from all walks of life for crimes ranging from DUI to homicide, the middle-five-figure income suddenly fails to satisfy, and the committed People's Advocate goes private, and immediately starts defending the rabble he or she used to send up the river. Like a star player who is traded to the archrival, not only does he know his old teammates, he's read the playbook! Memorized it. Dog-eared the important pages.

"Oh, come on, Wendell," you're saying, "It's not like that. It's not a game."

Yes, oh yes it is. I'm sorry to report that, in the final analysis of the Prosecutor/Defense Attorney relationship, it is merely a game. Haven't you ever watched a baseball or football game? At the end, when it's over, invariably some guys from one team can be seen on the field chatting with some guys on the other team, smiling, patting on the back, making plans for later, maybe get the wives and have dinner somewhere. Well, that's the way it is in your Court of Law. When the game is done, when the final gavel drops, time has expired and what's behind is just that, behind.

Well, it's the same with D.A's and Defense Attorneys. They go to the same pub after work and, sure, they jab each other. But in the last analysis, none of them is going to go to jail tonight.

The lawyer's argument reminds me of a child teaching a new game, one that he or his playmates made up. Only he really knows the rules. The student may try to utilize an option he has learned, only to find out that, in this particular situation, that option is not available. Throw something like hearsay up in front of a skilled lawyer (did I use that phrase?), and she will delve into the numerous, and I mean numerous exceptions to the Hearsay Rule, and spank the ball right back atcha. They love to argue and they hate to lose, but, no matter whether they win or not, they "win" at the bank. And, after a while of winning and losing, they will be satisfied with the fee.

A lawyer reading this book might be very angry now. He or she may try to find some way to either prevent further publishing of this book or, better yet, a way to sue this publisher or me (really both) to get money. Either way, when an insecure lawyer's nerve is plucked, he or she will take all steps necessary to stop the twanging. And you would think that this lawyer would be angry because of my unflattering portrayal. And you may think the ire stems from a deep love of the law, or what he or she may perceive as my ignorance, or frustration because I no longer buy into the lengthy line of crap.

But you would be wrong again.

This lawyer is angry not because I'm exposing the fragile and insecure world in which he or she operates with a sense of what she'll argue is dignity and professionalism, but because the mirror doesn't lie. She will look into this mirror I'm holding up to her and see herself, bathed in a sea of darkness, sullen and empty. Exhausted. Frustrated. Worried. It's not what the lay person sees; the lay person has known for years what I'm saying here. The lay person sees the legal profession with a clarity that only common sense can bring. They've *been* angry. They've *been* burned.

No, the anger that I've churned up in the lawyer here is the same kind that a kid feels when he realizes there's a "kick me" sign taped to his back. Because he knows something isn't right. He sees the looks. He hears the snickering. He is certain somebody is being made a fool. But when he discovers that the someone is him, well, he's mad. He's downright pissed. And many reactions can follow, each of which containing a certain amount of denial. The skilled lawyer-to-be tries a variety of arguments.

"I knew it was there all along."

"I put that there myself."

"I don't care."

 "I'll get the SOB who put that there."

But when he turns a complete circle to see every last face laughing with glee at his misfortune, and that nobody believes anything he has to say, that's when he's most dangerous.

He's trapped.

So which came first? The law or the kids and their "kick me" sign? Where did the first injustices incubate? When did Americans acquire this perpetual need to win? Who is responsible for all this competition, this conflict, this dispute-laden society? When did confrontation on all fronts become so avant garde? What I'm referring to here is the seemingly unending competitive streak found in all walks of life in all types of people. Neighbors, kids on the schoolyard, couples, drivers, consumers of all varieties, best friends, fathers and sons, landlords and tenants, contractor and contractee, siblings, rich, poor, famous and insignificant are doing battle with each other everyday. The arena may be different, and certainly the degree of commitment to the fight and the value of the spoils are far-ranging. But, like it or not, we seem to love to fight, because, I would argue, we need to win.

"Winning isn't everything," said old Coach Lombardi, "it's the only thing." That one sentence, revered by generations of insecure people in all walks of competitive life, flies so fervently in the face of what we were told as kids, and what we tell our own kids.

"It's not whether you win or lose, it's how you play the game."

To which those compulsive winners reply, "That's what losers say."

Think about it. We're so fully on our head as a society that most of us don't really believe anymore that it's "how we play the game." Deceit and fraud have become so deeply enmeshed in modern day business dealings that "how we play the game" and the soft pillow that comes with it have been easily replaced with winning as the only goal. The ends justify the means. In fact, deceit is so second nature that we scratch and claw and cheat and steal and take whatever necessary steps to win at work, then go home to our kids and issue the old mantra. We deceive them. Right after we deceive ourselves.

Shoot, even professional athletes will tell you of the myriad of tools the players use in order to "gain an edge" on the competition. Players in all sports will push the rules envelope as far, and even farther, than is allowed. Football players hold and pitchers scuff up balls and hockey players take cheap shots and boxers hit low blows and golfers use metal woods (sorry, that's a personal pet peeve of mine, but I still think it's cheating. I like to think of myself as coming from an era when clubs were wood and men were metal). "How you play the game" is different for everybody, I suppose. But deceit and cheating and gaining an unfair advantage in order to compensate for insufficient talent is a huge lie only to oneself.

The point is that deceit and misdirection and incomplete disclosure in order to achieve a desired result are so commonplace so as to be the accepted norm. Advertising, no matter the media, is fraught with lies, and we all know it. We've grown accustomed to or just tolerant of unbelievable claims and incomprehensible disclaimers that contemporary advertising is really just the National Enquirer of consumerism. Don't get me started on advertising; I could go on for days. Maybe the silver lining here is that the lies have created a savvier consumer, somewhere in America.

Politicians are simultaneously revered and defiled (*okay, maybe not "revered," but they are "celebrities," and, as such, get the red carpet treatment from a lot of people*). Every voter knows that as a politician on the campaign trail speaks, he or she is lying. Every constituent knows that his or her congressman or senator is under an unspoken order to avoid the truth. They are, as Jackson Brown so eloquently penned, "lawyers in love" with, ostensibly, money and themselves, not necessarily in that order.

And that brings us back to our brethren in the law. Lawyer-Politicians are, as we have seen, adept at saying the appropriate thing at the appropriate time, to the appropriate audience. Completely attired in the uniform of the day, the Lawyer-Politician says the right thing at the right time, whether it is compatible with his or her last statement, or, much less importantly, his or her own beliefs such as they are. Somebody, lots of somebody's, I suppose, correctly queried as to why a person would spend millions of dollars to be elected to a job that pays, at most, 200K a year? That absence of logic alone should disqualify them from public service, the kind of public service where they get to spend other people's money.

If you think of society as a pyramid, then the head or the top or the tip of the pyramid has to be the law governing that society. At first the Constitution and then the legal system that purports to uphold it. Within that portion of the pyramid are the practitioners who perpetuate the law. Underneath it all, and subject to all the fallout or, as I like to think of it, the wastewater, are The People. As in any organization, the law of gravity applies. Everything trickles down from the top. Good, bad, indifferent. They all find their way into the lives and the livings of those below. Perhaps there is a degree of evolution on the way down, or maybe a tempering, but whether the leadership drives a Hummer or an 88 Ford Bronco II, the people are chained to the bumper and have to necessarily go where it goes, eating all the dust and tar and vermin the road can deliver. (Alright, so I mixed up the metaphor there; the point is that at least some of the leadership's "stuff" gets on you.)

And you'd think that the leadership is the government, and you have to be at least a little right. But, above the government, flying around like the Goodyear blimp, is The Law. The Law sets the pace (which, as fortune would have it for me, is about as swift as the Goodyear blimp) along with which we the people walk. "Meander" may even be better. The misdirection here is that we get to call it a thing unto itself: The Law. Like "The Sun," over which we have no control whatsoever. And there it is. The genesis of the notion that, regardless of my position as a lawyer or a judge charged with upholding, interpreting and running The Law, it is still a fickle blind lady with a life all her own. Out of my hands.

And that, dear reader, is the big lie. The lie from whence all other lies come. The lie that created "reasonable doubt," and "malice aforethought." The lie that housed and fed the systematic shedding of one's own responsibility in favor of the tenuously related deep pocket. The lie that spawned and clothed a woman's right to choose to kill another person who just happens to be growing inside of her. At the end of the day, the lawyer throws his hands up in the air and says, "That's The Law."

Obviously, for most of us, that happy resignation is the worst cop out of all. It's ironic, isn't it, that if we all were approaching an intersection and simply removed our hands from the steering wheel and our foot from the brake, that the ensuing carnage would ultimately be sorted out by The Law? I mean, if The Law is some kind of barely controllable King Kong, why are we subjected to its wrath when we behave like it? Aha, see? Maybe the law isn't so uncontrollable after all. Maybe it's a very well-behaved Bengal Tiger just waiting for the command of its master, the lawyer. Then, when it one day goes berserk, the lawyer says, "hey, he never did that before," and the law and the lawyer get away with one bite. Put 250 years of "one bites" together and you have a shaky foundation of behavior upon which you have built an entire socio-economic nation.

Which is all well and good until the mid-20th century when we started shining a very bright flashlight on all the cracks and crevices, exposing the "design" flaws and holes to a world of critics and we got all defensive again. So, we beat up the world on two fronts, and super-powered ourselves into the techno age. But, we couldn't fix the foundation—in fact, we're only loading more on it and weakening it—so we fashioned a culture of leisure and entertainment for ourselves, to treat the symptoms of our weakened immune system—our Constitution—but still we fight. Still we compete. Still we need to win.

Lawyers, many I know anyway, have adopted an attitude of if you can't beat 'em, join 'em. The Law is huge and lumbering and spans centuries and cannot be controlled. I'm reminded of a scene in the original *Robocop* movie when the prototype robot doesn't obey the commands of the operator and riddles a guy with bullets. But, just like in that movie, one person can make a difference. Oh, not on a grand scale. One person isn't going to save the world. But one person can have an influence on the circle in which he or she operates. A father can have an impact on his children, a wife on her husband. You can be "salt and light" to your friends and neighbors. And one lawyer, who chooses not to fight anymore, even if hundreds wait eagerly to take her place, sends a message to somebody.

My mother always told me to walk away from a fight. A red-blooded American boy, I could not see logic anywhere near that suggestion. As I grew up, somebody told me I should choose my battles, and that seems like good advice. When the focus is on a solution rather than simply victory, human progress is made. Remove the love of money from the equation and there'd be a lot less fighting. Don't believe it? Let's tell all the pro ball players that the annual salary is now $50,000. See how many play just because they love it. You get a bunch of guys playing a game they love, you devalue the outcome. You devalue the outcome, you end up with a premium placed on how you play the game.

With the emphasis placed so much upon the outcome, people even go for things that they don't even know what to do with once they get them. I lost a lot of really nice girlfriends when I was a youngster because I coveted them so much for their beauty or their, well, beauty, I guess, and I worked very hard to win their favor. I worked so hard, in fact, that I didn't give any thought at all as to what I would to with them once I had their attention. The premise is again flawed. The thing of beauty, the object of an obsession or desire, whether money or fame or a win or even a girl, is assumed to be a worthwhile goal, a no-brainer what everybody wants. Especially money.

A lot of reasonable people, when asked what they'd like to have most, say "a little more money." Of course, a lot of people say "a LOT MORE money," but let's leave them for a minute. Reasonable people want more, but claim to not need too much more. Why? Why do people answer such questions with what the world would call a ridiculous answer? I think there are two reasons.

First, reasonable people realize that there are many valuable things in life one cannot acquire with money. Family, respect, honor, integrity, love, peace of mind, satisfaction with oneself, these cannot be bought. Our modern society has, of course, found ways around this truth by offering quite unsuitable yet widely accepted replacements for sale. For enough money, one can purchase a wife. Just like that. Thousands of women, desperate for the American Way of Life, offer themselves to generous American gentlemen willing to pay whatever price for permanent companionship. These are consenting adults, and to what they are consenting is a life devoid of the greatest riches afforded human being: love, happiness, trust, sacrifice, intimacy. For the purposes of this book, however, we must nod our heads a little in the direction of a Law that forbids prostitution yet facilitates mail-order marriages. And it's the same with adoption.

For decades there have been lawyers standing at the ready to prey upon the most vulnerable clients of all: Couples who cannot biologically become parents. Imagine, after a lifetime of searching for "the one," two people make a lifetime commitment to one another, and a logical next step for many is to start a family. I have sat with my own wife on two separate occasions when a fertility specialist looked her in the eye and told her she could never have children. Once the reality sets in, let me tell you, a woman will do just about anything to get her hands on a baby. Not that men don't feel the same way, mind you. But the maternal instinct is so strong in many women that the inability to bear a child is also unbearable. They will steal another's child right from the nursery at the hospital. They will go through a living hell and take drugs and deny and think about a surrogate and adoption.

Now, I've not been personally involved with the adoption process, but I've known many people who have, and I have friends who foster kids whose "parents" are in no way fit to raise these kids, and I've heard the horror stories. Acres of paperwork. Miles of red tape. Overworked, uncaring, uncommitted social workers who wade in the river of unwanted children everyday, many of whom don't themselves understand why it has to be so difficult to move an unwanted child into a loving, caring family. The process itself can take years and, if not carefully prepared and executed, can one day be subject to retraction. That is, natural birth parents are now using the legal system to retake custody of their once-adopted children. (See? We bounce children around like so many possessions and then wonder why our world is unraveling).

But the process can be streamlined and accelerated, for those who can afford it, by acquiring the services of an adoption lawyer. Now, here I'm not talking about the great men and women who assist two like-minded parties who wish to provide a permanent stable environment for a youngster whose own parents realize they cannot provide for him. No, here I'm talking about the swine who prey upon the young women who have no other place to go and who refuse to abort this precious life inside them. Lawyer nee baby broker. A young girl in need, a wealthy and willing couple and nobody gets hurt right? I have heard of prices as high as $100,000 for a healthy white infant.

So the degradation of a society of laws continues. The once-revered brothers and sisters at the bar, the statesmen and stateswomen who valued justice above money, are, like the brave men and women who liberated the world from the grip of Nazism, Fascism, Socialism and Communism, leaving this world in significant numbers each day, and leaving a vacuum which is being filled by "practitioners." Your new lawyers, like the law itself, are the product of a both a devolution of society itself, and the deflating acceptance of or resignation to the notion that one person has frighteningly little voice, and, after all, the auditorium is really quite vast. The law is pushing its practitioners along like a swiftly moving river, and it should come as no surprise that fewer and fewer have the spirit to fight the current, especially when balanced with the financial reality of the practice of law. Many of those who have recognized the situation for its painful truth have simply gotten out of the practice altogether, realized that the singular satisfying element to the practice of law, money, isn't really that satisfying after all.

As a nation of People, people subjected to the law—whether it be the criminal law or the civil law or administrative regulations or executive orders or regulatory agencies or municipal ordinances or homeowner's associations—every day, we ask ourselves the big question: Are we in too deep?

For the law, the simple answer is, "yes." Outside of an opinion by the Supreme Court throwing out well-entrenched doctrine such as punitive damages in a civil lawsuit or legalizing many recreational drugs, the law now has the most definite answers it will ever have. Each day that passes, each new precedent that is invented, finds the law further and further from anything that can be described as a tenet, or a predictable outcome.

Right now, right now, if you feel like a pilot in an airplane in heavy overcast unable to find a suitable landing site, good. That's how I want you to feel. There was a time in legal history when her lawyers took the clothes out of the dryer and ironed them neat and tidy and organized them on hangars in an orderly fashion, and we all appreciated that, even if we didn't love the exact arrangement. Not anymore. Driven to victory instead of a suitable conclusion that brings clarity, The Law only confounds and complicates, opening more wounds than it had at the outset. Myopic lawyers no longer fly overhead to see the big picture because they know the overcast never clears. Furthermore, a satisfactory result means the end of the gravy train.

Now you want me to tell you there is hope.

Truthfully, there is, but that hope is tenuously based upon People taking a reasonable approach to life, an understanding attitude towards one another, and a humble assessment of our role in society. Sure, there are multitudes of seemingly interesting items inviting us to vacate our well-worn pathway, distracting us from the ultimate prize, one we know to be satisfying. But the screams emanating from the edges of our periphery are but carnival hawkers interested only in confusing us into taking part in their empty schemes. Follow that voice too long and one will become a willing participant in a world in which the temporal rules, habitually jumping from one immediate gratification to the next. Soon, the careful, deliberate and disciplined journey is dispatched, relegated to the "if you can't beat 'em, join 'em" pile.

And the legitimate shedding of accountability that allows a lawyer to argue with feigned passion for opposing sides of an issue is just another cop out, another opportunity for a human being who happens to be a lawyer to justify his or her failure to take a stand and embrace the truth. For them, there is no truth. But it doesn't have to be that way for the rest of us.

I urge you to realize that one person can make a difference. No, not to the world, but in your immediate circle of influence: your family, your workplace, your place of worship, and with your friends. The Law will always be that convoluted destructive force seeking to divorce you from your common sense, but it is principled (not the best use of that word, I grant you) only by money. Once a person wakes up to discover (and one day you will, if you haven't already) that money is not the pinnacle the world has made it, the vast array of beneficial and valuable commodities life has to offer become the satisfaction in life that no thief can steal, and no lawyer can get a piece of.

Felix Frankfurter's Crazy Invention

While there have been a multitude of inventions that have withstood the test of time, most of them clearly relied upon natural laws, to the point of actually providing a means around, through, over or under matter. THE WHEEL, for instance. When people are intent upon leaning on a well-proven tenet or fact or law, they say, "Well, we don't want to re-invent THE WHEEL." THE WHEEL was an incredible invention, because it rolled. Rolling, we now know, was easier than all the other ways of getting around, or getting large heavy objects back to the cave or up on the hill. It was a good idea that, if blessed with sufficient momentum, could defy gravity. Simple. You know, if the wheel were to be invented today, the guy responsible for the project would be on all the talk shows for several days describing the process and the work work work to get the thing accomplished. I can see Jay Leno now:

"So, you've got this thing here, basically a round shaped object?"

"That's right, Jay," the guy pipes back, careful to use Jay's name to show that he's paying attention. "It's the round shape that is at the heart of the "Rolling Thing.' Our team worked for months to come up with the right geometry, and this design eventually won out."

Applause rings out and Jay shakes the guy's hand and the smiles...

But people were probably much simpler then, surviving and all, and they just wanted to find an easier way of doing things; if old Thog came up with the idea for the wheel, who the heck cares? Everybody benefits from it, right?

And there's flight. I love flying, and watching things that fly, and reading about things that fly. Most people credit a pair of brothers named "Wright" and a little place known to history as "Kitty Hawk" with the invention of "flight." Fact is, lots of people flew things before old Orville and Wilbur. Gustav Whitehead, for instance, flew a heavier-than-air craft powered by an engine as early as 1902, somewhere in Connecticut. The difference is—and the patent the Wright's hold—is that the Whitehead flyer could only go straight. The Wright Flyer of 1903 utilized what is now known as "three-axis" control: Pitch, Roll, and Yaw, which, along with Thrust and Lift, equal Controlled Flight. The Wrights patented it, three-axis flight, but not by flying in Kitty Hawk. It was a little place down the road called "Kill Devil Hills" where the Wrights first flew their glider and, later, on December 17, 1903, the powered Wright Flyer.

Inventions like The Wheel and Three-Axis Flight, as I have noted, are founded on the principal that Mankind's natural environment could be better navigated through the use of a device. And, even flight is simple, once you understand it.

Anyway, the problem for lawyers, when it comes to inventing new things is really twofold: First, they don't deal with natural laws. Secondly, there are no simple inventions in the law, which is why so few of them actually fly or roll.

Natural law is a beautiful thing. Sir Isaac Newton observed it, meditated on it, loved it. He was able to see it work, clearly in his mind, and write it down for us to one day question and criticize. But Natural Laws withstood such abuse, and now we know that an object in motion will tend to stay in motion, and that one action causes an equal and opposite reaction. Billiard players and racecar drivers and NASA and Lotto winners must abide by them. They are truly the great equalizers. Indian philosophers and spiritualists have applied Natural Law to the spirit or immaterial world and called it, "Karma." Karma, as you probably know, is the "science" of "what goes around comes around." And, I suppose, sometimes it does appear as if poetic justice occasionally prevails.

But in truth, there is but one Loving God who does not store up your bad acts on a ledger and then seize opportunities to regale you or repay your bad acts with equal misery. Nor does He keep count of your good deeds and then create a special place in Heaven to repay those as well. No, no bad act (by you) will earn you Hell, and no good act will earn you Heaven. If you've been burned by a lawyer and the preceding is an unpleasant surprise, remember that there is always Judgment Day…more on this later.

But, lawyers want to be the guy on Jay Leno, pumping hands and smiling and saying Jay's name. They want to be remembered for something, in one of those dusty books described in a previous chapter. Being on the Supreme Court isn't enough, you see. Having a name like Oliver Wendell Holmes or Felix Frankfurter isn't enough, either. Dreaming up a doctrine called, "The Fruit of The Poisonous Tree?" Now that just might do it. There's something very existential about it, something harking back to The Beginning…

Unless you are really unavailable, you have heard something about the story of Adam and Eve and the Garden of Eden, yes? Okay, so let's put that true story into perspective so you understand how to get to Heaven, and avoid Hell. God wanted companionship so He created Man, and named him Adam. God understood his own desire for companionship and therefore He gave Adam Eve. Good so far. Then, He gave them this incredible Garden full of every type of fruit and vegetable ever created, and animals and birds, and gave Adam (and, presumably, Eve) dominion over it all. There was but one catch, and most of us today would not have a problem with it. God told Adam and Eve to not eat of the Tree of Knowledge of Good and Evil, for if they did, they would surely die.

Enter Satan.

Satan says to Eve (*every man wants to make hay over the fact that it was Eve who was first tempted by the serpent, Satan, but Satan felt that he would have easier work with Eve, and he just knew that she would have easier work with Adam. And, like a burglar, Satan simply chose the best target for his master plan*), "You won't surely die. You will be like God and know everything, and God doesn't want you to know everything, because He's God." So, she ate and she gave some to Adam, and immediately they knew they'd made a mistake. A huuuge mistake.

The Fruit of The Poisonous Tree is sin, pure and simple. It's bad, and Mankind has sought for centuries, millennia even, for a way (other than the one God told us about) around and out of the effects of the Fruit of The Poisonous Tree. Anyway, the point is that everything that comes after the Fruit of The Poisonous Tree is sin, and without God's contingency plan, death. (*Now, the ACLU, to my knowledge, never challenged the naming of Frankfurter's Doctrine, but that was a long time ago, when thinking, caring, hard-working, believing people would never think of challenging the existence of God.*)

Frankfurter, however, has no such contingency plan for his Doctrine of the Fruit of The Poisonous Tree. Everything that comes after it means Death.

In order to understand the Fruit of the Poisonous Tree doctrine, you must understand the concept of "admissibility," and why there is a Fourth Amendment to the Constitution in the first place. The Fourth Amendment was written, generally speaking, to prohibit unlawful or unwarranted searches and seizures.

"The right of the people to be secure in their persons, houses, papers, and effects, against unreasonable searches and seizures, shall not be violated, and no Warrants shall issue, but upon probable cause, supported by Oath or affirmation, and particularly describing the place to be searched, and the persons or things to be seized."[14]

The Framers of the Constitution and its amendments were all too familiar with the nasty habits of the soldiers of The Crown who, armed with (at the most) some gossip, would approach the home of an unsuspecting colonist, say, about three A.M., bash the door in and perform a thorough search for contraband or evidence of espionage. As you might suspect, given either the rather global disdain for The British Empire held by the colonists or some underhanded misdirection by Her Majesty's Finest, said evidence was usually found. Once the evidence—the map or the notes or the guns or the whatever—was in hand, the man of the house was often requested to out his compatriots or, worse, to confess to being a sympathizer.

You see, the trouble plaguing the British during the decade preceding the Revolution was nothing more than a resistance to Imperialism. People living rather humble lives in a beautiful and fruitful environment—and wanting to keep it that way—were merely defending their land. Many were simple farmers and fishermen. Others were rabble-rousers and resistance organizers, of the type the British wanted to eliminate. Trouble

14 Amendment IV, United States Constitution

was, they had no idea who was who, not to mention the fact that the Motherland was thousands of mile away.

So, they walked around and they listened and they paid silver to informants who, with little in the way of scruples, pointed a bony finger at whomever, and the soldiers barged. Sometimes, as I have alluded to above, they were wrong. Unable, however, to accept such an outcome, soldiers regularly carried contraband and evidence of espionage along with them, and planted it. Then, they would beat or coerce a confession out of the poor sodbuster, rape his wife and daughters, slaughter a calf or a lamb and eat it, and, maybe even burn down the cabin.

Flash forward 200 years. In the year 2001 stories are still being unearthed, literally, about American G.I.s in Viet Nam, overcome by war and all her assorted nasty parasites, practicing a little shotgun warfare of their own. Unable to discern friend from foe, they became adept at emptying an entire hamlet of her civilians, searching huts, burning huts, and, as horrifying as it may be to accept, slaughtering men, women, and even children. (Only recently did this same United States put to death one Timothy McVeigh for the sick and unbelievable slaughter of 168 men, women, and children in the bombing of the Murrah Federal Building in Oklahoma City, a terrorist act he likened to an assault of war.) It is all so Karma-esque that people tend to believe in the notion that history repeats itself. The point is, we don't want something that apparently regularly happens in wartime to occur on a regular basis in the civilian world.

And that's why we have the Fourth Amendment. Protecting for two centuries the rights of honest folks to be safe and secure in their houses and "effects," the Fourth Amendment has a noble heritage. Like so much of what is "American," it owes its existence to a crisis, and the lack of thorough planning on the part of the either naïve or uncourageous Framers has created a heyday for a legion of hair-splitting litigators.

Because then came the "Fruit of The Poisonous Tree" Doctrine.

To paraphrase Drew Carey and his description of drive-through liquor stores, the Fruit of the Poisonous Tree Doctrine is "almost a good idea." Frankfurter coined the phrase in *Nardone v. United States,* 308 U.S. 338 (1939), and stated simply it says, if a search warrant isn't "warranted," then everything in the case that is discovered or uncovered or obtained as a result of the "bad" warrant rises to the level of evidence obtained as the result of an "unlawful" search and or seizure, and is therefore unconstitutional and inadmissible as evidence against the suspect. All of it must be excluded as evidence from the trial. Period. A gun found at a residence of a suspect, found due to a bad or incomplete search warrant, must be excluded. The names of co-conspirators or a witness and his or her testimony, discovered as a result of a bad warrant must be excluded. And, my all-time favorite, a confession derived from a suspect who was apprehended as a result of a warrant later determined to be unwarranted, must be excluded.

Now, In the *Nardone* case, the evidence used to prosecute Mr. Nardone was obtained through the use of illegal phone taps which were in violation, at the time, of a Federal Statute (the government didn't think it was included in the group of people who couldn't use clandestine wiretapping). Ironically, that law was written to lend statutory language to the words of the Fourth Amendment, presumably because the Fourth Amendment wasn't clear enough on its own, as though electronically knocking down the door was somehow different from physically barging in. Anyway, Frankfurter painted with a broad brush in his Fruit of The Poisonous Tree Doctrine, and the criminal defense bar has never been the same.

You say, "Wendell, how can it be that a guy confesses to killing three nurses in their dormitory while they slept, and later have that confession ruled invalid?" How indeed? Remember, I'm the guy who used to stand up there and defend these guys. I'm the one who used to lean on old Felix's doctrine anytime I could. And now I'm saying, sometimes the ends DO justify the means. NOW I'm saying, yeah, okay, so it was a bad warrant, but we've got the guy and he's confessed so, hey, let's find a way around this silly, outdated, ridiculous doctrine and its prodigy. You think I'm Right Wing? Wait until the guy who raped and killed your daughter goes scot free on a technicality under the "not perfect but the best judicial system in the world." Go ahead, blame the police, everybody else does. But I've seen the police work, methodically, within the lines, trudging frustratingly along in search of that elusive prey: Probable Cause.

Now, "Probable Cause" is the Policeman's Holy Grail. Probable Cause is the key that unlocks the Warrant. He or she will not make a move without it. A cop can know that a suspect is the perpetrator of a crime, maybe he even has some evidence to prove it. But until he takes the step to link his evidence to a Probable Cause Search and/or Arrest Warrant, to take a suspect into custody is the same as walking away and doing nothing to solve the crime. Why? The Fruit of The Poisonous Tree. No Probable Cause? No Warrant. No warrant, no nothing that you get from the suspect after the arrest (like a confession). See?

What makes a warrant bad? Lots of stuff. Warrants must be sworn to. "I saw so and so steal a purse and then run into a certain apartment, and not leave again," is classic warrant language. (Now, if a cop saw it, she wouldn't have to get a warrant, because of something called "exigent circumstances," meaning that because a cop saw it and some evidence may be destroyed before a warrant can be issued, the cop can establish her own probable cause.) Usually, however, a cop will swear out a warrant based upon eyewitness testimony or that of a C.I. or "confidential informant." Many judges will not require a policeman to reveal the name of his C.I., but some will. In either case, a C.I.'s testimony is suspect since the reason he or she is a C.I. is because he or she is known to be a criminal, usually with a long record, and agrees to become a C.I. in order to avoid jail time. Cops routinely pay C.I.'s as well. But warrants can be bad because of a vague description of the thing to be seized, or even a poor description of the place to be searched.

We definitely do not want innocent people to be the subject of a warrantless or unwarranted search. But the Fruit of The Poisonous Tree Doctrine wasn't written in response to an unwarranted search of an innocent. Instead, it was written to spank a government for using illegal tactics to gain a conviction. Legally collect evidence, get some testimony, get a warrant, bring in the bad guy, and roll him over. That's the way it should be done, and that's what the Court was saying. Belt and suspenders. But the Doctrine was out of the bag already, and then the lawyers got hold of it.

This Doctrine is the devil behind those cases you hear of having been "thrown out on a technicality." A missing colon, a mistyped address, a misspelled name, a questionable scope of the warrant, questionable credibility of the witness, etc., have all led to cases being dismissed and bad guys going free. Lawyers did that. But there's more.

For example, a warrant states that the police can "search the residence at such and such an address," and the cops search the house and the garage, and find evidence in the garage (the victim's torso, let's say). Upon finding the body, they promptly arrest the owner, and bring him in. During the interview, let's say he agrees to a blood sample which ultimately links him to a dozen other murders. When asked about them, he confesses to all 13 murders, and gives a detailed statement about each, including where to find the bodies.

Now, along comes an F. Lee Bailey-type and he points to the warrant and says the garage is not the residence. (Shakespeare's Shylock said a pound of flesh didn't include any blood, remember?) Old Frankfurter or one of his contemporaries agrees, says the cops "exceeded the scope of the warrant" and tosses it out and, because of The Doctrine, heaves the entire case out the window. The cops have the bodies, and they certainly know whodunit, but they can't prosecute because of an aberration, an anomaly dreamed up by one foolish lawyer thinking he was doing a good thing, and exploited by another who, were he to call upon his long ago-jettisoned humanity, would observe that he most definitely is not.

And that's how the law, written in response to one crisis, and based upon a Constitutional Amendment written in response to another crisis, becomes absurd. A serial killer sent out to kill again, and a criminal defense lawyer who believes he has helped humanity and the American Way Of Life by defending the Constitution, as interpreted by an old coot with either no vision or no conscience and little common sense. Sure, Frankfurter was a Federalist, and was just making sure the Government was kept on its toes. But all he really had to do was rule that the statute banning wiretapping included the government, and the case would have been the end of it. Instead, he wrote an encompassing doctrine that has given logic and common sense a drubbing, and finds crime victims and a sympathetic public, who only want justice, now seeking vengeance and retaliation against not only the perpetrator of the crime, but the abetting Law.

I believe, in the entire spirit and scope of things, that the Framers of the Constitution had something else in mind when they wrote the Fourth Amendment. I'd like to think that, based upon the demographics at the time, the Framers could not possibly have envisioned a United States so full of hatred and bitterness and mistrust. So here's a bombshell for you: I believe they meant to protect *Actually Innocent People*. I think that, when they wrote the simple words of the Amendment they would never have imagined that somebody, someday, would actually use it to allow killers of The People to go free. Of course, The Doctrine isn't the only way killers get away with murder. But it sure is the most popular and the most economical.

I spoke with one lawyer about the Fruit of The Poisonous Tree Doctrine, and he began a lengthy diatribe heralding the lofty ideals of The American System of Justice. "Better ten guilty go free," he began, chanting the Defense Attorney's Mantra, "than one innocent spending even a day in jail." Well, I've defended them. Let me tell you, I can recall only one "innocent" in my entire career.

I'll call him "David," and he was all of eighteen years old. David was a straight-D student who never really had a steady girlfriend. He didn't ever have much to say, but when he did, at least to me and to anyone I ever heard him speak, he was respectful and sincere. The sum total of his firearm experience lay in his love of rabbit hunting in the woods behind his house with his old mutt dog and a .22 Remington long rifle. A simple kid from Kentucky who excelled at working wood with his hands, David was really no more than a lanky child who spent his school days in the wood shop. In most other areas, he was clueless, but none proved so life-changing to him as his inability to say "No" to his much older half brother, "Earl."

In the late summer of 1989, Earl, 39 years old and mean, was paroled from an Ohio state correctional facility after serving 19 years of a life sentence for the first degree murder of his parent's elderly neighbor during a home invasion. The very first thing Earl did was steal a car. He then drove himself to a truck stop on interstate 75, and flipped a coin. Unfortunately for David, it was tails. Earl headed south.

Somewhere between Cincinnati and Lexington, Earl robbed a McDonald's restaurant, brandishing a .357 magnum handgun. He then proceeded to the home of his father and half brother, David. Earl hid out there for a few days, taking the time to become re-acquainted with his sibling, who hung on every word Earl uttered, especially of his tales inside the "joint." David wasn't even born when Earl was convicted and sentenced to prison, and had only heard passing stories about his "black sheep" brother. Only after meeting him did Earl take on a humanity to David that David found alluring. Earl was flashy, matter of fact, quick-witted and charming. David had just graduated high school and had little in the way of life plans, so, when Earl suggested young David accompany him on what Earl described as a job exploration trip in Tennessee and North Carolina, David jumped at the offer.

The crime spree began in Kentucky, where a convenience store clerk nearly paid for her protestations with her life. Somehow, Earl's .357 missed the middle-aged woman, and the two ran out of the store.

There was something about McDonald's that Earl found very attractive, and it wasn't the Big Mac. They were, at the time, quite easy targets for armed robbery. In Pigeon Forge, Tennessee, Earl and David grabbed a bite, and then demanded money from the clerks. After obtaining what amounted to a little over $100, Earl directed the clerks to the rear of the store, where the manager was doing books. With the muzzle of the .357 up against the young woman's head, Earl demanded she open the safe, which she was thankfully able to do. The pair took the two-thousand dollars or so, and began to exit, but Earl decided there were too many potential witnesses, and he bludgeoned the manager almost to death, firing a couple of shots into the ceiling for effect.

The two men then drove like the wind into Western North Carolina, and hid out at a state park near Canton. While there, Earl opened up a duffel bag and showed David a cache of weapons including a 12-guage shotgun and several hand guns. For a couple of weeks, Earl and David hid out and spent money on everything from expensive jewelry to prostitutes. Running low on funds, they located a pawnshop near Asheville. Earl told David they would try to pawn some of the guns.

They arrived at the pawnshop around ten in the morning, and Earl showed the 22-year-old manager some of his guns. "Kevin" examined the weapons and totaled up a price he was willing to pay for them. Earl either scoffed or told Kevin he would think about it, and the two men left the shop with the guns. David's statement told what happened next.

"Earl said, 'did you see that wad of money that kid had in his back pocket?', and I said, 'nope.' Earl kept saying that that kid had plenty of money, and why wasn't he willing to pay more than a hundred dollars for them guns and did you see that wad in that kid's back pocket? We drove around for a while, got some lunch at a barbecue place and Earl kept talking' about that kid at the pawnshop. I says, 'why don't we try another pawnshop?' and Earl just smiled at me and told me to shut up, that he was thinking. Then, about three in the afternoon, Earl asks me if I saw anybody

else at that pawnshop and I says, "nope," and he says, 'maybe that kid will give us more near closing time.' So Earl finds a payphone and calls the shop and asks what time they close and the kid said six, I guess, and so we decided we would go back about closing time.

"When we get to the shop, Earl gets out the 12-guage and a .22 pistol, and hands me a .22 pistol too, and tells me to put it in my pants, behind my back. He puts his .22 in his waist band in front and covers it with his Redskins windbreaker. We walk into the store and the kid sees us and says he's about to close and Earl says, 'can you please see if you could give more for this Winchester?' and by that time we were standing in front of the counter and Earl puts the 12-guage down on the counter and reached into his waist band and pulls out his .22. I see the kid reach into his pants pocket where there was a bulge and Earl says, 'don't try it buddy,' but the kid pulls out a pistol but before he can get it all the way out Earl fires at the kid, twice, and I pull out my .22 and take a shot at the kid too, and he puts up his hand as he's fallin' backwards on the floor and I was just about to reach over the counter and shoot him again, but a huge explosion went off and the counter shattered where the kid fired his .357 up at us. After a couple of minutes with my ears still ringing from that gunshot, Earl goes around the counter the other way and looks down and the kid's not moving or nothing, and Earl reaches under him to get to his pants pockets and pulls out a wad of money. The kid was bleeding all over the floor and not breathing or anything and I says to Earl, 'you think he's dead?' and Earl says, 'let's get the (heck) outta here' and we book it. I don't even think I hit the kid, but Earl sure did."

I argued like a madman to get David's statement excluded. He was a hapless companion to this demon of a half-brother, and he was in almost every sense only along for the ride. When the police lab examined David's little .22, they found that the remaining 10 rounds were blanks. I decided to go after the physical evidence in attempting to get his statement regarding him shooting the weapon excluded, based upon the impossibility doctrine. This doctrine required both for David to believe that the completion of his alleged crime (homicide) was impossible and that it was physically impossible.

In this case, however, the judge ruled that David had no knowledge of the non-lethality of his weapon and therefore the defense was incomplete. It would have been fruitless, however, since North Carolina has the Felony Murder Rule, which basically states that if you are a party to a felony and, in the commission of that felony somebody is murdered, you as the felon are guilty of murder. The classic example is that of a convenience store armed robbery in which a policeman aims at the perpetrator and fires his weapon, but mistakenly hits and kills another innocent individual or, for that matter, an accomplice to the crime. The felony perpetrator is guilty for the murder. I argued viciously for the judge to understand the mental state of David, and that he was not a willing participant, based upon his statement.

The problem with the entire matter was the identity of the victim. "Kevin" was 22 years old, the son of the shop owner, and the former star of the high school football team. He was well liked and had never, to anybody's knowledge, so much as stolen a piece of gum. He was in the church choir and was probably a virgin. From a Defense Attorney's standpoint, he was the worst possible victim. After the trial was all said and done, David was convicted and sentenced to serve the rest of his life in prison. That, you may find incredulous, was a victory. The state had wanted the death penalty, both for he and Earl. For a Public Defender, keeping a kid out of the gas chamber is a huge victory. Keeping this kid, guilty of murdering the perfect young man, out of the gas chamber was tantamount to a miracle.

I had the sensation from the beginning of this case that David was no killer; when I found out the bullets were blanks, I wanted so badly to send him back to Kentucky to start over. But he was the only one in hundreds I can recall that I ever felt that way about. True, he was present when a murder was committed, but he was, in all definitions of the word, "innocent." What does this have to do with the fruit of the poisonous tree? Good question.

The car that the boys used to get away was found crudely painted yellow, taxi-cab yellow. The police stopped it late one evening because some of the paint had dripped over one of the taillights and obscured it from view. The officer was on a routine traffic stop. He asked if he could look into the trunk, because, he said, the car, except for the paint, matched a description of one used in a hit and run. He was just lying. Having nothing incriminating in the trunk, Earl quickly agreed. When the officer opened the trunk, he saw the obvious interior color of the trunk and decided the car had been painted to hide its identity. He made further inquiries and decided he had enough to perform a search of the vehicle and called for backup (you see where this is leading?). On a search of the automobile, the police found some money, and the guns, and arrested the two on illegal weapons charges. Once in custody, David was tricked into giving a statement about the pawnshop murder, and the police used his statement to charge Earl.

My argument (and that of the appointed counsel to Earl) was simply one of a warrantless search. The men had agreed to a search of the trunk, which yielded no real evidence to further the search to the rest of the vehicle. We almost had a dismissal when the prosecutor suddenly found a case in Delaware in which the State Supreme Court decided that a differing paint job in a trunk on a car that otherwise fit the description of a "crime car" could trigger probable cause. But remember, the officer had made up the story about the hit and run. This made no sense to the trial judge, who simply said that the police have to sometimes use "tactics" to fight crime.

The Appellate court held differently, however. That the officer had fabricated a crime in order to further his search was an unconstitutional abuse of discretion, and that Probable Cause nor Reasonable Suspicion was never evident. Curiously, the Court decided that David's "voluntary" statement was not connected with any unwarranted search or seizure, and it was still a good confession. Nobody in North Carolina ever had the money or the time to take this one to the U.S. Supreme Court, which is another in a long list of tragedies in a tragic case. On retrial, the jury found the two guilty again, but this time sentenced Earl to the death penalty. David is still in the North Carolina Penal system.

The real crime here is that somebody who most lawyers admire, and many of those who are not lawyers recognize his name, created the law out of nothing in order to satisfy his own sense of right and wrong in a single legal case before the U.S. Supreme Court. "Legislating from the bench," is what it's called, and these days it happens at seemingly every session of The Court. The dizzying labyrinth created by two-hundred years of the Federal Judiciary, melded queerly to fifty individual and significantly differing state judiciaries, is replete with contradiction and nuance, and therefore holds precedent for nearly every politically-motivated viewpoint emanating from the Highest Court in The Land. I cannot remember the last significant majority ruling, i.e., based entirely upon well-established precedent. Nearly all opinions handed down by the Supreme Court fall neatly along party lines.

Many people don't fully understand how the Court operates.

The United States Supreme Court is made up of nine justices, appointed by the President and confirmed by the Senate. Naturally, although it shouldn't be this way, the President will appoint justices he believes share the President's political ideology. That's one political hurdle.

The U.S. Senate conducts hearings, both at the committee level and at the full-Senate level (if a candidate makes it out of committee), with questions to the candidate that are designed to divulge how the justice will rule in any given politically charged legal case. Usually, everybody knows if a candidate is going to make it to The Court right from the outset. If he or she is a strong conservative judge, and the Senate is in democratic control, that candidate is likely to fail to be confirmed. Liberal democrats are fearful of confirming a justice who may vote to overturn *Roe v. Wade*, or who may have strong Judeo-Christian morals and will help stem the tide of secularism in the United States.

But that's not where the politics end. Say our candidate is confirmed. After he or she arrives at the Court, there is the case selection process.

Many people believe they have rights that they simply do not have. For instance, some people think they have the right to a driver's license, but, in fact, this document is a privilege and not a right, and can be taken away from you without due process of law. Another right people think they have is the right to be formally charged of a crime or be released. In fact, a person can legally be held for 48 to 72 hours without being formally charged with any infraction. I say "48-72" because Justice Sandra Day

O'Connor, in her opinion on the matter, never did clarify that time frame. She only said that two weeks was naturally too long.

The big right people believe they have, and that they don't at all have, is the right to have a case appealed to the U.S. Supreme Court. Yes, you have the right to *petition* the Court to hear your case, but your chances are very slim. Truth is, out of the over four-thousand petitions the Court receives each year, it agrees to hear only a handful. Those cases are carefully chosen for one of two reasons: Either the Court is going to use a case to further solidify a loosely held tenet, or it is going to overturn a verdict, again, to attempt to clarify The Law. The Court is usually not going to hear a case of "first impression," that is, one in which The Law is totally unfamiliar. The Court will likely pass on these cases unless it feels strongly one way or the other. In *Roe v. Wade*, the Court sensed a real threat to anti-federalism and therefore knew it had to act (more on Federalism later).

Legal inventions like the Fruit of The Poisonous Tree Doctrine are at the heart of why The Law is a failure. Sure, there is a semblance of predictability (an anomaly in the law for sure), and yes, such a doctrine imparts some knowledge to law enforcement. But, as we can see here, it often flies in the face of logic and, perhaps more importantly, common sense and, most assuredly, Truth. A nation forced to succumb to the whim of an illogical and irrational Law is not a representative democracy or a nation of The People; it is a dictatorship.

THE RIGHT TO LIFE

The Right to Life.

Such a foregone conclusion, it is amazing that the words even have to pass over the lips. Certainly, human beings have some sort of Right to the essence of what makes them human, living organisms. A cell divides, and that act is duplicated millions upon millions of times, geometrically, for 42 or so weeks, and the result is another one of "us."

Utilizing the "miracles" of modern science, we watch. A kidney bean with a heart beating at light speed slowly becomes a kidney bean with feet, hands, eyebrows, a face, a brain. He or she laughs, burps, sleeps, dreams, kicks and punches mom to prepare her for the sleepless nights to follow. More than procreation, the endless repetition of life giving life giving life is not merely at the core of the reason for our existence (and the irony or hypocrisy of that statement is not lost on me, mind you), but it is the reason itself. It *is* the core!

The point is, it happens, life. Somehow, within the feeble operating systems that are human life forms, it happens. Why in the world would anyone ever attempt to determine whether one has a certain "right" to it? I mean, how silly is that?

There are those, even among the family of believers, the faithful if you will, who hold to what I see as a skewed belief system regarding the "tales" of the Old Testament. The stories of Adam and Eve and the Garden of Eden, Noah and his ark, Moses and the Red Sea, Abraham and Isaac, Jonah and his whale, all of them, according to these "believers," are but fables told and retold through time in an effort not to fool or even convince, but to represent to the inferior human mind the power of God Almighty and to prepare us for the miracles of Jesus, which they do, reluctantly, seem to believe.

I am not one of these people.

I believe in Adam and Eve, Noah, Moses, Abraham, Jonah, you name it, if it's written in the Bible, I believe it. I can't imagine that people who label themselves "believers" can be so disbelieving. I now breathe a heavy sigh and return to the thrust of this chapter from my digression, although you will see it is not without reason.

I believe God made Adam in the image of Himself and His Son, Jesus, and the Holy Spirit. God said, "Let us make man in *our* image." God is the author of all life and He made Adam as part of His master plan for all creation. As a result, I tend to think of God as Life. God *creates*; it's what He does.

The Founding Fathers acknowledged God in everything they did in their own creation of the United States of America. They noted, not cloistered in any politically correct manner, that human beings were endowed by The Creator with certain inalienable rights. The first of which occurs as the Right To Life. Until that time, nobody had actually said it out loud, but declarations and constitutions being what they are, namely the writing down of what a group believes so that its leaders and its followers will be fully informed, it had to be written down.

Now, despite not being a part of the Constitution itself, I argue that the Archives can be taken as a whole, and the Declaration of Independence was the gateway to the Constitution. Like the introduction to the book you are now holding, the Declaration is a thesis, or an encapsulated statement of what you are about to read. Later, after you've read the book, you can go back to the beginning and re-read the introduction to see if what you read in the text of the book seems to follow what the introduction said.

It is so complete in its vagueness that one has to wonder why they even went on. A songwriter like Jim Croce or Carol King would have been completely at ease with the Declaration and went with that alone. My point is that the Declaration and the Preamble to the Constitution were obviously written for the People, because most of The People at the time would have been incapable of really understanding what came after them.

Anyway, why argue over the Right To Life if, after all, it's written right there in the Archives? Sitting down? The Declaration of Independence has no legal weight. Again, the People—you, me, Croce, King, probably Dan Fogelberg and Lennon and McCartney—all outside the Constitution looking in. Why? By now you must know: We Are Not Lawyers!! It's true, I was a lawyer, and, in all probability am still accurately classified as a "Lawyer" if not an "Attorney at Law," but I think by now you see that I have completely jumped ship and am back among the living, breathing, and, most importantly, the feeling.

The document that is the Constitution is and was written only for lawyers. While the Declaration purports to set forth the "inalienable" rights and the rules for making us "created equal," the Constitution is first and foremost the backbone of the invertebrate that is the American Judicial System, a place where you and I are generally not welcomed unless represented by an attorney. There is much more on this topic later. Suffice to say for now that the Right To Life so eloquently set forth by Mr. Jefferson himself is not guaranteed by the Constitution of The United States. Yes, the Declaration and Preamble make it very clear why there even was a *need to write all this stuff down,* namely *because we're alive and have a right to be alive and here's how we should live our lives!* Without life, and a guarantee to it, why even have a Constitution? I mean, if it matters not if we are alive or dead, then why go to such extremes, such headbanging in that little room in Philadelphia in order to so thoroughly *protect it?*

Let's say a bunch of guys get together and decide that they like playing golf soooooo much that they are going to put their heads together and have a club. They write a long list of rules, a book really, and every member has to agree to the rules. Without golf, why have the rules? Okay, maybe a stretch. Maybe not.

Which is why, 230 years later, we are at war in this country over the very reason we have a country in the first place: We Are Living Beings and We Want To Protect Our Way of…LIFE.

In 1972 the United States Supreme Court heard arguments in the case of *Roe v. Wade.* "Jane Roe" is the clever feminine synonym for "John Doe," and was given by the courts to protect the Plaintiff's real name, which we all now know is Norma McCorvey. Wade is the last name of Henry Wade, the Dallas county District Attorney. This case is well documented and has been given more press than the Second World War, but I feel like you need to know the case and its arguments a bit more so that you can see how the Right To Life became a main subject of political candidates' questionnaires for the past thirty years.

Texas had a state statute banning abortion, and McCorvey thought that was wrong and unconstitutional and sought to overturn the law so she could abort her unborn fetus. She made the argument (*ever notice how we tend to characterize the arguments and legal strategies as if the client birthed them?*) that she had the right to her own life, to make decisions about her own body, and that the state had no right to tell her what "medical procedures" she could have on her own body. For them to do that, she said, meant she had no right to privacy.

Now, in order to fully understand this case, one has to fully appreciate the socio-political climate at the time. First and foremost, this is the heyday of the sexual revolution. Women have championed the right to make their own decisions about what would affect their lives, thanks in part to men doing a miserable job of doing so for so many years. A major reason for this failure is the slow, subtle but steady removal of fathers' influence on their sons' lives due, in large part, to the Industrial Revolution of the early twentieth century. Once dads were carted off the farm and into the cities for a daily grind of prog-ress-driven, mind-numbing work, moms were in the unhealthy position of being the primary care-giver to their sons, and that major feminine influence induced confusion in boys, leading to a deep insecurity.

Insecurity, by nature, seeks security. Boys who grew into men became so fixated upon finding that security that we looked everywhere to find it, often resulting in unhealthy alli-ances and associations that produced, in many cases (similar to Adam's), abject failure in personal and leadership roles. Once men's ambivalence towards these roles became fixed in society—and when women left the home to seek their own professional identities—men's logical influence took a back seat, especially in matters that, on their face, seemed inherently feminine, like abortion. All this confusion of roles and blurring of boundar-ies led to a burgeoning sexual freedom that, as one might guess, spread like wildfire.

Sexual freedom, fueled in part by the overall emergence of a societal freedom which found its voice thanks to the Viet Nam debacle, meant women had more control over their bodies, and were no longer "chained" to the morals of a generation which had so thoroughly failed in terms of global politics, the environment, the struggle to ease racial relations, and a whole gamut of other social, economic, and political arenas. JFK was murdered by communists, despite McCarthy's witch hunt, and a generation of empowered American young people sought out its own leaders: Abbie Hoffman, Jimi Hendrix, Timothy Leary, Hunter Thompson, Hugh Hefner. Helen Reddy sang, "I am woman, hear me roar..."

The organization of women, fully half of the entire population, could not escape the attention of politicians eager to remain employed. Congressmen, Senators, and Presidents found themselves unable to count upon the "good old boys" for re-election, and were forced to reach out to the female voter by speaking her language. In simple terms, that meant a few things: child care in the workplace, equal pay for equal work, and, the big one, Reproductive Rights. By the time the early seventies rolled around, the Supreme Court had been sufficiently sculpted so as to respond favorably to the Plaintiff in *Roe*. The Court did an end-around a variety of Amendments and arrived, by a 7-2 margin, at a conclusion that supported the liberal political leadership and completely rocked the world. A woman had a right to kill the baby growing inside of her.

(The Court even circumvented a well-entrenched tenet of the Appeals Process—the concept of "mootness"—and decided that the gestation period of a human being being necessarily finite, McCorvey was not required to even still be pregnant when the Court heard her case. Let me clarify. If a plaintiff's case is or will be "moot," or irrelevant, by the time the appeals court hears the case, then the case cannot be heard since that court cannot issue an order that can be enforced against or for a party. In Norma's case, the Court was unable hear her case until after she had already delivered the baby, so it should have declined to hear her case based upon mootness. Instead, due to political pressure from various directions, including on the Court itself, the Court wrote down some mularky about pregnancy's inability to outlive the appellate process and suspended the mootness test for this case).

In other words, in just under 200 years, the United States went from being One Nation Under God, to a nation entirely in the grips of sin, and the Evil One himself.

I know the arguments. I used to be an opinion columnist for a local Asheville North Carolina newspaper. I rather often utilized my space to flog Christianity, morality, and the Right To Life. I said that the "right to life ends at birth," when the right to own an assault rifle, and the right to a death penalty take over. I said, "*Whose* Right to life? A productive, adult member of society, or an unknown fetal commodity?" I actually wrote that. I said that Pro Choice was merely the power to choose life it you wanted it, not the right to only choose abortion. I said that adoption was the latest commodity for sale to the highest bidder, and that adoption was available only to the wealthy and most stable of citizens.

Worse than writing these things, I can say without any hesitation, was arranging for and participating in the abortion of two babies, my babies, my baby boys. Living. Breathing. Hearts Beating inside their mother. One in 1987, the other in 1990. Two separate occasions. That's one occasion, replete with all the heartache and suffering and guilt and calamity that goes with it (certainly enough to discourage a *repeat*, you would think) followed only a couple of years later by a second. On purpose. Can there be a more vicious killer than me?

Lest you think my campaign against abortion is fueled by my own guilt, let me make it clear that, although it took years of therapy and prayer, I know that God has forgiven me. Guilt free, but never forgetting the pain and anguish that accompanies the snuffing out of human life at its most vulnerable, innocent age. But let me tell you about the peace.

What makes God so great is His never-ending mercy and grace. Nobody you know has that. Nobody is able to watch you, love you for years and years while you never learn from your mistakes. Nobody will stand there and let you listen, understand, and then take a completely opposite pathway, *and still be there time after time when you realize, once again, that you have flubbed up.* And nobody will ever forgive you for requiring her to kill her baby. And certainly not *two* babies. Believe me.

But God does. Over and over again, His mercy is truly infinite. Does He like it? Of course not. He is saddened each time you fall. But He's God so He knows your life even before you ever lived it. "Before you were in the womb, I knew you." Can you get what I'm saying here? No, you can't. I can't. The limitless grace of God is not to be comprehended, only accepted and with endless gratitude.

Who knows how and why people flip? An anointed minister in California named Jim Jones, loving, caring spiritual leader of the people, led his flock to a Guyana jungle where his faith fled and left him empty. He filled it with drugs and sex and descended into the embrace of Hell itself, taking 913 lives with him.

Perhaps the people of the world are bombarded with so many conflicting messages from a variety of media that they remain in a constant state of conflict and confusion. After all, that's what Satan wants, it's what he's best at, confusion, division, separation. If he can keep your mind on the trivial of the world long enough, you'll eventually lose sight of the prize, he knows that. He'll take an intelligent mind with a weak will and convince one of an absurdity.

I saw a hypnotist giving a demonstration once while I was in law school. He invited students chosen from the audience completely at random to come to the stage, ten or twelve of them, and, one by one, he hypnotized them into a variety of humorous modes. He made one girl believe she was entirely naked. Another fellow would, upon the issuance of a code word by the hypnotist, stand before the crowd and sing "I'm a Little Teapot" while spanking himself. A third student was asked if he knew the Gettysburg Address. He answered that did not know the entirety, only the first few words. The hypnotist counted to three while pressing a finger to his head and the young man's head drooped to his chest, and his eyes closed. The hypnotist then said that the man would, upon hearing the word "Lincoln," recite in its entirety the Gettysburg Address, and would do so in Lincoln's voice. He did, and what's the point? That the human mind is weak, and that the human constitution is weak and the human is weak. So saturated with television and everything it fires at us, we have given up the ability to think critically, to question, unless we're told to. Absurd, isn't it?

What I'm about to say concerning the legal system is at the very root of why it doesn't work, so bear with me. When I was a kid, a friend of mine convinced me to do what he was doing. We were on a sidewalk in the center of town and he was simply looking upward, but seemingly focused on a single thing in the sky. I did so, and we laughed, but he said don't laugh and I stopped. Soon, some passersby saw us looking and stopped to look as well. Not wanting to be rude, I guess, or maybe afraid of appearing foolish (beautiful, isn't it?) many didn't ask what we were looking at. If somebody did ask, my friend simply pointed upward and said, "that thing, there. You see it?" or something like that. And even though they didn't see it, they said they did. Soon, a crowd formed, but I couldn't keep from laughing and the people caught on that it was a gag and the crowd dissipated.

Well, in a way, the law is like that thing we weren't looking at. And the lawyers are like my friend and I. The crowd is the people blinded by the seeming legitimacy of the law. And this book is like me laughing.

A pretty well known sketch on the popular show, "Saturday Night Live" was entitled "Unfrozen Caveman Lawyer." In this sketch, Keerock, a Neanderthal man who was brought back to life after being encased in ice for thousands of years, becomes a lawyer. His impassioned jury summations include references to his inadequacies and unfamiliarity with the modern world, but those do not prevent him from knowing with all full knowledge, "...that my client deserves one million dollars in damages, and one million dollars in punitive damages." It serves to poke fun at a couple of well-known lawyers, but also bitingly shows that people will stare at nothing if the right person in a seemingly legitimate environment says something is there.

Point is, what began as a system of establishing the manner in which we should live life overstepped its boundaries. Now, the legal system not only is in charge of determining whether there *is* a life, but also whether or not it will continue to be one. A system with that much power should frighten you.

Back in the *Roe* days, some argued that allowing a mother to abort her baby would begin a slippery slope towards a place where the Law would have more control over the lives of the innocent. In *Roe*, the viability question was raised and answered in the affirmative: even a viable fetus could be killed if not doing so would endanger the life of the mother. Imagine that? What mother would allow her baby to be killed so that she might live? Well, now we know that there are some 40 Million mothers with that kind of willingness, each with a skewed interpretation of the word "live." And the slippery slope predicted all those years ago? Well...

On June 4, 1990, Dr. Jack Kevorkian, using a crude machine he crafted consisting of $30 worth of scrap parts scrounged from garage sales and hardware stores, injected Janet Adkins, a 54 year old Alzheimer's patient, with a lethal dose of drugs. Jack Kevorkian killed Janet Adkins, plain and simple. In the back of his Volkswagen van. Kevorkian argued that he was doing Ms. Adkins a favor, and because it was what she wanted.

Kevorkian had a proven obsession with planned euthanasia, writing articles in medical journals and establishing himself as a 'death counselor' during the 1980's (obviously years after abortion on demand was rubber stamped by the Supreme Court). He logically reasoned that if life was a selective event at its beginning, why shouldn't it be so at its end? Why, if mothers and fathers have the right to determine if a person lives or dies before it is born, can an individual not have the same rights over his or her *own* life? On the heels of *Roe v. Wade* the logic is unassailable.

Dr. Kevorkian, having assisted in over 100 suicides, was eventually, and I mean *eventually* convicted of second-degree murder, and went to prison. But the legal war waged in Michigan over the course of ten years made many lawyers very wealthy and famous. And, true to form, once the law really got its hands on hot moral and ethical issues, it wasn't long before the words became so commonplace that critics and commentators forgot entirely about the lives of the people the Law was impacting.

I'd argue that one of the biggest reasons for the devaluation of life has to do with the apparent decline in the quality of life due, in large part, to the ever-present oppression of the Law in American society. Around us every day we see countless examples of hopelessness, depression, anxiety and defeatist attitudes, often the result of the Law. I mean, one single DUI (*not, of course, condoning drinking and driving here*) can cost over $6,000. The numbers of DUI offenders is staggering, due, in large part, to the heavy-handed lobby known as MADD, the Mothers Against Drunk Driving. Thanks to this astonishingly powerful lobby, the legal blood-alcohol limit in most states is well below .1 per cent. That means that an average sized person can enjoy a glass of beer with dinner at a restaurant and be already over the legal limit on the drive home. That wouldn't even mean much if we weren't bludgeoned to death with alcohol advertising everywhere we turn.

But the psychological ramifications of a single DUI can run quite deep. If you were to lose your license, which, by the way is entirely possible, you may lose your job. Lose your job, lose practically everything. This one unbalanced law contributes to so much pain and suffering in our society, and that's just *one* law, folks.

Thanks to instantaneous worldwide information, the law goes much deeper into our lives than that, too. The media hounds us with atrocities against every sort of person, countless stories of aberrant behavior by everyone from common criminals to upstanding members of our communities, churches, governments and the Law. Images of natural disasters, widespread famine and disease, thoughtless acts of lawlessness, and decadent behavior by individuals who have been elevated to celebrity status permeate our daily lives. Our minds are in a conundrum as we are locked into a paradox of images: Lifestyles of the rich and famous with innumerable toys and evidence of their wealth on one hand, well-established underworld gangs of young people lashing out at a world in which they see no future on the other. Unwinnable wars being waged in some parts of the world while a legion of tourists enjoy tranquil tropical vacations in others.

It is life, and it is death, and it terrifies us to the point of being at once fearful of death—and what it may hold after—and sometimes unable to find a reason not to hasten it. I ask my customers in the barbershop how they're doing today.

"Well, I'm on the right side of the grass, so I guess that's something," is the reply, or something to that effect. Truthfully, I often say, "well, you never know." For Christians like myself, life (as we know it) is but a blip on the timeline of eternity, which is how long we believe we actually "live." No, not in this world, but in spirit together with God in Heaven until there is no more time. Why, you may ask, would someone who believes so richly and fervently in everlasting life be so concerned with *this* life, or this part of life?

And I wish I had the answer. As Christians, we have a faith that even though we don't have all the answers, we know who does. And that's the comfort that gives us hope to "keep on keeping on," in the face of a world that finds less and less to be hopeful for every day.

But I digress again, because now that the decision to live or die at *either* end of life has been bestowed upon mankind, there remained only one area in the life or death question that remained. The Law was salivating.

Terry Schiavo was a healthy, active and employed 26 year old who, on February 25, 1990, collapsed in her home with a cardiac arrest. When her husband found her and called 911, paramedics tried unsuccessfully to resuscitate her. As a result, her brain was deprived of oxygen for a significant period of time. Terry remained in a coma for two months, eventually awakening and entering a period of cyclic consciousness/unconsciousness that continued for the rest of her life. The legal battle surrounding Terry's case consumed some 15 years and presented the courts with a number of life and death issues revolving around both her present medical condition and conflicting accounts of Terry's degree of viability. Additionally, there existed violent clashes between a variety of family members and friends regarding Terry's personal wishes for continuing to live under these difficult circumstances.

The legal battle zigged and zagged for a decade and a half, with her husband, Michael, making dozens of attempts to have Terry removed from life support, and her parents, Bob and Mary Schindler, using every tool—legal, political and in the press—at their disposal to block those attempts.

Terry Schiavo was alive. She breathed on her own, and her heart beat without assistance. The only type of real life support she was on was a feeding tube and, in March of 2005, Michael was ultimately successful in obtaining a final court order to have that removed; Terry starved to death two weeks later. Read that sentence again. *A court ordered a living, breathing human being to be starved to death!*

Okay, okay. You want to give people the right to die when their old and dying already? I'm not going to say 'alright," but I'm not going to argue the logic. You want to give moms the right to kill a child growing inside of her? Well, that really makes no sense to me at all, but still, there are arguments that have to be called 'logical' (if not right) in support of that idea as well. And I realize there are ways in which an individual can make preparations for the unfortunate day when he or she may end up in a state of suspended animation, being kept alive only through the magic of modern science. I'm not granting that these are acceptable, only that, in the grand scheme of life and death, one could argue that these decisions aren't entirely illogical.

But killing a *living breathing human being??* You gotta be kidding me. But here's the kicker. Absent the court's decisions in *Roe v. Wade* and the Kevorkian debacle, Terry Schiavo would still be alive today. And who knows, maybe she'd be walking around and eating on her own and and and.

But we'll never know, because the decision to live or die is no longer in the hands of the One who created us, but in the illegitimate hands of those He created.

CLASSICAL MECHANICS AND THE LAW

To say that Isaac Newton was a genius is trite, I suppose. The man who gave definition to the movement of bodies through space and invented Calculus no doubt earned a certain unspoken and unique place of honor in the circle of historical great thinkers. True, he remained a virgin until his death. And yes, perhaps he was a bit difficult to abide at times, even by his closest friends and admirers. There are other stories detailing his eccentricities. But nobody can deny him the label "Genius."

To me, the true genius of Newton is how his laws for the physical world often transcend into the non-physical. Maybe Newton realized the universal potential of his discoveries, and I'd like to think even he was able to recognize the manner in which the physical could dominate the emotional and the mental, especially when it comes to human behavior. But maybe he missed the connection entirely.

Newton's first law of motion is simple: *A body in motion tends to stay in motion, and a body at rest tends to stay at rest.* Our retired racing Greyhound, Lord, is a good example of this law. When he's galloping full tilt, legs reaching, pulling him at speeds near 40 miles per hour, let me tell you, his 75 pounds tend to stay "in motion." But right now, at four o'clock in the morning, he's here at my feet and he is truly "at rest." Okay, his digestive system seems to be working overtime, but he's down for the count.

The law is kind of like that. On the surface, it may appear that it is at rest, not moving, static. The wheels of justice do, indeed, turn slowly. But inside the "machine" a lot is happening. Innocent people are being devoured by hungry lawyers; cases are being digested at alarming rates; and the "law" that emerges at the end often stinks worse than even Lord's gas.

The reason it stinks is simply because justices, judges and lawyers won't leave it alone. Forget about impartiality, or that justice is "blind." Every person in the inner workings of the law has a private agenda, and he or she knows that patience, determination, and being prepared to do whatever it takes will get that agenda passed. Okay, refresher from chapter one: Remember who your lawyers are? Right! They are the insecure, power-hungry crybabies pulling each other's fingers and stabbing each other's backs. It doesn't take a Newton to calculate the private agendum of this group. Think of the law as a billiard ball travelling across the table. Each time a judge notices the ball going toward a naturally acceptable pocket, but away from his private agenda, he strikes the ball with one of his own balls. Now, he's not going to hit the ball so hard that it goes off in entirely new direction, or, God forbid, back in the opposite direction. Judges don't want to call that much attention to themselves, nor do they ever, ever want to be overruled by the Appeals court. He "massages" it just enough so that it achieves the result he desires.

Now, multiply that minute mis-direction or I'll even say "re-direction," times ten. Or fifty. Or a hundred. Because, every time a judge gets her hands on a precedent, she alters it ever so slightly such that it isn't discernibly different, but it's not really the same as it was intended to be. The difference is sufficient to include her own prejudices or personal opinion in a certain case that is before her, and she may therefore utilize the presiding case to support her private initiative. Now, you've got what once was a ball headed for a perfectly acceptable direction (in the universal balance sense of the law) going God knows where. This ball, had it been allowed to keep on course, would have dropped neatly into a pocket where it belonged, where it was intended to go.

In the grand scheme of things, and in the law, it would be better (albeit sometimes with an initial sting) to allow things to follow their own destiny. Life would take on a certain certainty, a predictability that follows the bulk of the population's common sense. The sense of security and regained trust in human nature would allow the world to return to an order not seen since the 1950's, and, like it or not, most of us would be much happier. Judges are simply not about sitting back and taking it all in, I'm afraid. So, our judge gets her way by massaging an already lukewarm precedent, and it seems as though nobody gets hurt. But like the rock in the stream, the effect on the law by judicial activism erodes the necessary precedent so it becomes neat and smooth and spherical alright. But, We The People clearly need at least *some* jagged and sharp and angular law, law we can grab hold of and sink our nails into.

Nevertheless, the law bounces or erodes or is sloughed off over time, and the results can be irrational or, at least, unreasonable. And reasonableness is the first test in the law.

Take for instance that whole 'for every action there's an opposite reaction' notion. In fact, Newton's second law of motion states, *"For any given force or action, there is an equal and opposite force or action."* Newton surmised, correctly, that the energy of an object moving through space (any atmosphere or lack thereof) created an energy against the object that was measurably equal to the force of the object. An automobile hitting a brick wall is a good example, although Newton probably never imagined it that way. The car, travelling at 30 miles per hour strikes the wall directly on the perpendicular and the wall sends that 30 miles per hour force in directly the opposite direction. The result is the failure of a portion of the integrity of one or both of the objects. (Now, Einstein came along and said that the energy created and rapidly dissipated by the collision had to go someplace, which is why we have seat belts today, but I digress).

In the law, Newton's second law of motion is evidenced every day in many levels. From a simple lawsuit to far-reaching Supreme Court opinions, the clashing of "bodies" is the way the law is shaped. One party files a lawsuit, and the other answers. The second party *has* to answer, or the first party automatically wins by default. Like tennis, if you fail to hit the serve back, you lose the point. The Law (I capitalize here to distinguish between Newton's law and THE LAW) is adversarial *in nature*, not by design, even though it would be easier—not to mention more fun—to deconstruct if it were the latter. And, as we have already seen, the adversarial *nature* of the law is what gives her architects an unassailable scapegoat; in theory at least, one cannot sue Mother Nature (*don't think it hasn't crossed the minds of the more creative members of the bar.*).

Think about it. What makes a good boxing match? Sure, I do so enjoy a searing knockout. Watching a man (or woman anymore) take a neck-snapping swat to the chin and seeing his legs completely disobey his mind's commands to remain steadfast, while he takes the Nestea plunge to the canvas, another sack of potatoes for the pile, has a certain orchestra-like beauty all its own. But anybody will tell you that a "good" boxing match is just that: a *match*. Swapping blows, taking the upper hand and relinquishing it, neither combatant overcome for any discernable amount of time, a round won, a round lost, therein lies the true artistry of boxing. We love the *quid pro quo* of good competition, or at least we did. More and more, we as a society clamor for more career-ending KO's, figuratively speaking. Simple, quick, decisive and undeniable. But, lawyers say, *where's the fun in that?*

A lawsuit has a kinesis that follows Newton's second law in an uncanny fashion that cannot be coincidental: Lawsuit-Answer. Motion-Motion. Discovery-Response. Question-Answer. Verdict-Appeal. Award-Remittitur. Settlement offer-Acceptance. But, you see, somewhere outside the province of the latter, which is based in compromise, there is finality. An action without a reaction. A force without an opposing force, at least not within the boundaries of the law. Where does the response to the final force go? Perhaps the litigator saves it up and infuses it into the next lawsuit. A more plausible result is that it seeps into society, rearing its head in the media's ink, and out of the mouths of so, so many talking heads, and even in the pages of the book you are holding. Isn't that what this book really is, a *natural reaction* to the action of the Law?

The inescapable conclusion of Newton's second law is that the universe ebbs and flows, bobs and weaves, thrusts and parries, knits and pearls its winding way on a never-ending journey towards balance. But the cry for justice is *also* a cry for balance. Symmetry. King Solomon said, "To everything there is a season," a God-created order. But, to paraphrase Gerry Spence from his book, *With Justice For None*, we Americans put in our fair share and want back *more* than our fair share. It's what makes us Americans. On a daily basis, we upset the natural balance of things. We put our money in a variety of accounts and expect interest. We put in our eight hours and expect, and often get, the pay for fifteen. Or, more often than not, we work about five hours and get paid for eight. A corporation gives us a good salary, benefits, maybe an expense account or a company car, vacation, profit-sharing, and all it wants in return is our heart and soul 24 hours a day. We marry and pledge ourselves to another, and give ourselves to our spouses, but it is sometimes insufficient, perhaps based upon our "more than our fair share" experience. We seek out the companionship, or friendship, or love of another. We pay a paltry sum each month to social security so that one day, when we are still fully capable of earning a living, we can stop working and get paid a tidy sum far exceeding what we have paid in simply for having lived and worked. What a country.

Social programs like welfare and unemployment insurance upset the balance. Like so many inventions, these programs, created as stop-gap assistance to a hurting workforce, have evolved into a crutch, upon which rests a subculture of adult children from whom responsibility has so often been removed that they simply know no other way. And, while it may seem crass, advances in medical science have taken us to the point where life can be sustained indefinitely. Having spent our entire lives wanting—and getting—more, we are simply unable, or unwilling, to see it come to its natural end. We try to create fairness where fairness is not only non-existent, but dangerous.

In the law, we are injured through the carelessness of another, and we sue for damages. But we are not satisfied with just damages. We are not satisfied with being made whole, or as whole as can be. We want blood. We want revenge. We want to hurt someone the way we hurt. We want to take a few extra blows while our opponent is already buckling to the canvas.

We want *punitive* damages.

We want *more*. We lash out at our opponents, knowing full well that it or he or she or they are well insured and we go for the "deep pocket." There is a reason police officers refer to their line-of-duty mistakes as "jackpots." It is the lottery, except the odds of winning are frighteningly better. Insurance companies, being good stewards of the bottom line and knowing full well the real costs of protracted litigation, often settle cases that could easily be won. Money is king.

People stay in dead-end jobs simply because of the security and steady pay. Never mind that they spend a good portion of that income on creature comforts that are no more than painkillers for their aching souls. Eventually, a good portion of these disgruntled workers acquire on-the-job back injuries and Carpal-Tunnel Syndrome and get paid for doing nothing, and the thought that they are upsetting the natural balance of things, like their now-overworked co-worker, never crosses their minds.

So the tremendous irony is that we, as physical beings in a physical universe, have within us a primeval sense of balance and order, yet we are "gifted" with a free will that allows us to accept or reject the instinctual—and far-reachingly more beneficial—desires that accompany such order. The Neo-Classical model of the universe was comprised of a larger, infinite space in which mankind occupied a tiny, almost-insignificant speck of earth. In the two hundred years hence, the model has flip-flopped, and mankind is the dominant feature. The result of that 180-degree shift, fueled by the social revolution of the latter part of the twentieth century, is a greater attention to the self; we're in the "me" generation. (*See, even in the larger sense of the span of humanity, we see a pendulum-like example of Newton's second law. We have seen a world of communities become a world of individuals. Moreover, there are those who would argue that there has recently begun a shift back to a greater awareness of the need for family, community, and sacrifice for the good of the whole*). On a much smaller scale, however, the effects of an upsetting of the balance are much swifter.

A nation watched the hazy videotaped images of what seemed to be four white police officers mercilessly beating an unarmed black man who was mostly prone. It was horrible. The man begged, pleaded, and still the cops beat him. Eventually, the four officers were charged and had their day in court. Unfortunately, and most probably due to the special relationship between police and prosecutor, two were acquitted. An acquittal in a criminal case has a unique finality not found elsewhere in the law. The Constitution prevents double jeopardy or, "be[ing] subject for the same offence [*sic*] to be twice put in jeopardy of life or limb."[15] The equal and opposite reaction came like lightning. A community cried out. Racial tensions exploded. A city burned.

That may seem like a very strong example. I suppose it is, but it's not isolated. And, it's not as though events unfold like that every day. But, on a much smaller scale, yet no less painful or destructive, justice is denied with little or no legal recourse all the time. As long as we endure a legal system that ignores its victims and rewards those inhuman enough to exploit its fairly obvious weaknesses, the balance will remain upset.

Look at the At-Will Employment Doctrine. The notion that an employer has the right to terminate an employee at any time for any reason or no reason (provided that reason does not violate Title VII discrimination mandates) is rooted in the—again, Newtonian physics here—twentieth century's response to organized labor. Most labor scholars and historians will tell you the same thing about labor unions. Labor unions were a necessary and valuable reaction to the nation's first wave of bloodthirsty capitalists. At the latter part of the nineteenth

---

15 U.S. Constitution, Amendment V.

century, the labor breakdown in the United States was roughly 80 per cent agriculture, and twenty per cent everything else. We were farmers. We were born on farms and we grew up on farms and our dads and moms (and grandpas and grandmas) were right across the field. We got up early and worked hard and went to school, even though nobody really knew why, and came home and worked hard and collapsed in bed. Long hours were a fact of life.

When gasoline engines and concrete buildings and smoke and steam and iron signaled the ushering in of Industrialization, we left the farm and went to the city and had no reason to think we shouldn't awaken early and work hard, long hours and go to bed day after day after day. We were accustomed to it.

But Industrialization brought with it something else: The American Dream. An income stream meant we could buy things like a house of our own and one of those motor cars and a television, etc., etc., etc. But what good is it to have one of those kinds of lives if there's no time left in the day to enjoy it?

I don't know whose idea it was, but it comprises the very fiber of the working stiff. The eight-hour day. Somebody looked at the day and decided, perhaps existentially, that we should break it down into three parts. Sleep, work, and everything else. A 24-hour day naturally breaks down into three eights, so there you have it. Sleep. Work. Enjoy the "fruits of our labor." Our own tidy trinity.

But, owners of companies making cars and dresses and glassware found that their jobs required something more than eight hours, and they naturally demanded more of their essential workforce. People of all ages, lured to the city by the promise of independence and self-sufficiency that only money can buy, worked. And worked. And the harder they worked, the more time that was demanded of them. Then one day, somebody noticed that there were hundreds of workers and only one boss. And, I suppose they noticed that the boss wasn't all that sweaty and had nice clothes and a fine auto and a good house and his kids went to school instead of working, and they said, "Why is that?" The only logical reason could be that he had the money to enjoy his life. And, despite having nothing to do with the creation or the idea or the financial savvy or the courage to lay it all on the line and start a company from scratch, the workforce demanded its slice of the owner's pie.

"Cut back our hours," they clamored.

"No," he simply replied.

"Give us more money," they screamed.

"No."

"We'll all quit at the same time leaving you with nobody to build all those cars you've already sold," they extorted.

"Oh," was all he could say as his brow furrowed.

Okay, working conditions were waaaaaaaaay sub-par, and people were getting hurt and sick, and young children were in the thick of it, and wages were low, and some owners didn't care. We have them to thank for the twenty-thousand-dollar price on a regular old car. Now, because of the existence of the labor union, an unskilled worker on the assembly line in Detroit, who spends her day attaching wheels to Chevvys, earns more money in a year than a pharmacist, or a registered nurse, or a school teacher.

Labor unions flourished during the first half of the twentieth century, mainly because the largely unskilled workforce wanted the good life, and hadn't the power to obtain it on its own. Unions made sure that the working conditions were safe, and that a man (primarily) made a fair wage for a reasonable number of hours. But, just like the guy who has those in-criminating pictures of you and your neighbor's wife, unions became intoxicated by the power in a big money environment, and the demands became greater while productivity remained the same.

Or lessened.

Empowered by the market-driven demands of a nation wanting goods, unions preyed upon management's absolute need for a satisfied and loyal workforce, and extracted all but a morsel of profit from those to whom they owed a debt of gratitude. Unions became so powerful, primarily in the indus-trialized Northeast and upper Midwest, that many trades and professions were simply closed to any but dues-paying, card-carrying union members. In many states, that meant, virtually, all trades.

Why bring it up? Because the artificial constructs envi-sioned and created out of greed and a lust for power, all on the ruse of a better way of life for working stiffs, not only violated the majority of the people's notions of natural law, they did so *legitimately*, and with such order, that they have actually be-come the natural to generations of blue-collar families. Like I've said before, when I was a kid, Ricky and Lucy slept in their own beds. Nowadays, if a young T.V. couple out on their first date doesn't end up in bed together that night, *that's* unnatu-ral. As a youth, I used to listen to these old "coots" talk about a good day's work and earning their pay and the soft pillow it provided them, and I thought, "What bunk! Why work harder than you have to?" Well, that's my generation's mantra, and you can see where that's gotten us. Computers were supposed to free up our time, and just the opposite is true (I'm digressing again, at least I think I am).

The At-Will Employment Doctrine, adopted in virtually (*hate that word*) every state says simply that, in the absence of a contract to the contrary, and provided it doesn't violate any Federal Discrimination law, an employer can terminate employment for any reason or for no reason at any time. True, most of the latter statutes also include exceptions for an employer who utilizes this doctrine to silence a whistleblower, or to jettison a worker's compensation claimant, or for going on jury duty. But the teeth of the Doctrine is that it allows an employer to have more control over the workforce, again. It's a complete one-eighty from the organized labor movement, and really only dyed in the wool unionists think it's a bad Doctrine. It *had* to occur in order to try to achieve the natural balance. But it never would have occurred if employers didn't recognize that organized labor would ultimately destroy anything but service-related employment. Of course, as it is, employers have done a bit of back-pedaling themselves, establishing factories in cheap-hard-working-labor environments in places like Mexico and Singapore, and we're back to the roaring twenties all over again. What will happen when these twenty-first century third world employees organize?

The point is that there is a natural order to things, a rhythm and sequence in which life achieves its own balance. Action-Reaction. The Law has upended, even perverted that order in pursuit of the capitalization and exploitation of all that is in its control, which is substantial.

And there's no stopping it.

And that should frighten you.

"Leveling The Playing Field"

One phrase I think is overused, and has been for probably fifty years, is "leveling the playing field." Thinkers, some of them even great thinkers, over the last several decades have attempted, perhaps with the best intentions, to put teeth to the phrase from the Declaration of Independence regarding all of us being 'created equal.' To them, created equal means something more than being gifted with 'inalienable rights,' something more than the "pursuit of happiness." To them it means only "happiness." That somehow we, being fortunate to have been born a citizen of the greatest country on the face of the earth, should be able to avail ourselves—each of ourselves—to anything we want, regardless of our inability to pay, lack of talent or skill, or our cavalier attitude towards effort and hard work.

To these thinkers, it was unthinkable that, in this great country, one child may be more gifted than another—say, faster at the hundred yard dash. There had to be a way, they felt, to 'level the playing field.' Again, to paraphrase our friend Drew Carey, it was almost a great idea.

What really happened is that somewhere during the 1950's, child psychiatrists began to question thousands of years of successful child-rearing techniques, criticizing those techniques as 'archaic' and unprogressive. The world, they said, was changing rapidly, and children were becoming 'more aware' of themselves (due, in large part, to a growing cadre of 'enlightened' parents who believed that an 'evolved' society should banish the 'barbaric', albeit highly successful, practice of corporal punishment in favor of 'reasoned' discipline involving talking. Oh, and listening. And, you see where that's gotten us). This heightened awareness in our children meant that they were somehow engaging in regular patterned behavior of self-examination, and were becoming confused, frustrated and downright depressed at what they were finding. The answer, according to those great child psychiatrists, was to provide an educational environment in which the focus was to be moved from one of "unhealthy competition" to one of raising levels of self-esteem. Competition in the classroom, they said, left some children out of the educational loop. Certain socio-economic factors in a rapidly changing world were placing undue stress upon certain children such that they were unable to concentrate in the classroom, and teachers and administrators, spurred on by a left-leaning political environment—a 'we are the world' created-equal-ness—had a choice to make. They decided to remove the "pressure" of competition in the classroom. Towards that effort, some schools did away with walls around the classroom, standard seating arrangements, and time-tested teaching methods. But, chairs placed willy-nilly in a "learning space", "move at your own pace" lesson plans and pass or fail grading systems resulted in no structure. In the twenty-twenty hindsight of many, the decision was tragic.

The problem? Simple: Children are not as stupid as we think they are. Try and level the playing field on them, and they are acutely aware of what you're trying to do. They know they are not equal. They know one is better than another. You can't fool them into thinking they're they same simply by providing the same reward for different results. The point of leveling the playing field was to encourage participation by those children who had grown to feel disenfranchised due to, the 'experts' said, competition. It could not simply be that some kids just don't crave competition like others. It could not simply be that the subjects of said competition just happened to be of the type at which certain kids did not excel. A simpler "solution" could have been to just create different types of competition that reached out to more kids, engaged their minds, exploited their collective forte. See, the problem wasn't competition; it was the limited focus of it.

Earlier I said that if we diminish the importance of winning, then more importance will be placed on how we play the game. And that's true, but only to a point. We can't entirely remove victory and her spoils from the equation, no more than we can entirely remove how we play the game. Minimizing the importance of victory at any given task is exactly what we're talking about here. The winner of the Olympic gold medal in pole-vaulting has achieved an admirable goal; he has not achieved the only admirable goal, not by a long shot. Why in the world would we want to either take away his achievement or divvy it up between all the participants?

Have ten kids run the 100 yard dash. Afterward, give each of them the same "prize". Do that enough and pretty soon, there's no incentive for the fastest runner to try to win. Pretty soon, there's no incentive for anybody to even run. It's as simple as that.

And that's not the worst part. The worst part is that children lost respect for themselves. If a person has no respect for himself, he certainly has no respect for anybody else, or anybody else's property, and psychologists and the Law have a name for people like that: Sociopath.

The Law has, in many instances and in a variety of arenas, codified the notion of leveling the playing field. At first, the law and the cases arose from the Equal Protection clause of the Fourteenth amendment. That amendment conveys the protections of the U.S. Constitution to the States, and therefore prohibits discrimination by state government institutions. The clause grants all people "equal protection of the laws," which means that the states must apply the law equally and cannot give preference to one person or class of persons over another. What that really means is that an *existing* law must be equally applied. What it never meant is that a *new* law must be written in order to cater to the certain whim of a certain protected class of people, or for its benefit.

But look what happened.

Although the landmark 1954 case of *Brown v. Board of Education* effectively desegregated public schools, desegregation wasn't happening fast enough to satisfy the liberal elitists who are smarter than us all, so they took cases to the courts all over the country which resulted in busing. Black students from perfectly acceptable neighborhoods, albeit perhaps not as financially secure as some white neighborhoods, were bused to attend schools in the more affluent, predominantly white neighborhoods. Conversely, white students were bused to predominantly black schools. Do I have to tell you how this situation worked out? I'll always remember the uproar in Boston, because that's where I lived. And I'll always remember the snapshot on the cover of *Life* magazine of a "concerned" white father attempting to impale a black father with an American flag.

Well, it's the seventies and you know what happened. White girls started to get abortions and black girls would never get abortions and the once white neighborhoods became a mix of black and white and then predominantly black and then the white people left the community, the so-called 'white flight'. It is important to remember that the citizenry was never in favor of desegregation. The citizenry had enjoyed the life it had, with its neighborhood schools and neighborhood groceries and neighborhood churches. I'd never argue that there is no racism; only that forced integration fed the fire of racism, but I'm really digressing here. The point is, the Law has done very poorly at leveling the playing field.

Casey Martin was a good golfer. He was, in fact, a good professional golfer. It was his job (Sport as profession is a topic for another book, but how ridiculous is it that we pay millions of dollars to athletes and 40 grand to a school teacher?). All parties agree that Martin was of potentially PGA tour caliber. Unfortunately, Martin suffered from Klippel-Trenaunay-Weber Syndrome, a congenital, degenerative circulatory disorder that manifested in a malformation of his right leg. This disorder caused Martin severe pain and atrophy in his lower leg, and he was unable to walk for extended periods of time. The mere act of walking subjected him to a significant risk of fracture or hemorrhaging. Even the most nonchalant of those who have eyes know that, in the game of professional golf, one must do his fair share of walking. Sure, in the game of amateur golf, there are golf carts aplenty and a disabled amateur golfer can even disregard the rule to keep the carts 30 feet away from the green and drive right up to the edge of the thing, get out, putt, get back in, drive on to the next tee box.

But in professional golf, rife with rules, the PGA Tour decided long ago that golf courses were meant to be walked, and the game would be played by walking golfers. In 2000, Martin brought a lawsuit against the PGA Tour under the Americans With Disabilities Act, saying that it had to make reasonable accommodations for his disability by providing him with a golf cart.[16]

---

16 *Martin v. PGA Tour, Inc.*, 984 F. Supp. 1320, 1321

The theory of the case was that, since golf was his vocation, his "workplace" had to be fashioned to fit his disability, like wheelchair access ramps at the bank or grab bars in the men's room. Now, you're thinking about this and wondering what's the big deal? Give the guy a cart because he's disabled, that's the law, isn't it?

You say that because the years of subtle changes in the world around us, the years of tiny shifts in the paradigm from "life as we know it" towards that unattainable and even more undesirable level playing field have led you to a logic that defies logic itself. Fly overhead and look down. You're saying that a professional *athlete* should be able to compensate for a congenital lack of raw talent and/or physical ability. Would you give a beat cop a wheelchair because she couldn't walk? Would you force the horses to run slower to allow a stuttering track announcer to catch up? If I have a congenital disorder that prevents me from swinging a baseball bat quickly (which I suppose I do), would it be fair to ask Roger Clemens to slow it down a bit for me?

It is admirable that Martin overcame the bum wheel to achieve what he had achieved in the world of golf. But allowing him to use a golf cart tainted the game, caused deep, long-lasting riffs between able-bodied players and the Tour, and, in the last analysis, provided Martin with no quantifiable assistance. Cart or no, Martin could not play the game of golf at the level necessary to remain on the PGA Tour.

No doubt, someone will or has written a book about the personal struggle of Casey Martin, how he overcame the obstacles and the challenges and the criticism and won. His personal victory, while admirable, could not have been accomplished without a greedy, logic-defying Law whose lawyers are the ultimate victors, earning perhaps millions in legal fees off this one ridiculous case.

But the campaign to level the playing field invaded other areas of life. Affirmative Action is nothing more than busing in the workplace, and in the educational system. The term "Affirmative Action" was coined by President Kennedy (what a surprise…his nephew, twenty years later, invented the phrases "physically challenged" and "differently-abled" to describe crippled people), and was seen as a pro-active move to make civil rights a reality, to level the playing field for what appeared to be a legion of unfairly treated minorities. Basically, Affirmative Action sought to force employers and educational institutions to hire and admit percentages of minorities into their workforces and classes consummate with the identified percentages of those same minorities in society. On the one hand, the result, it was said, would be more opportunities for blacks and other minorities to become upwardly mobile in corporations and professional life. On the other hand, the 'diversity' would open the eyes of a "racist white society" to see the colorful nature of mankind first hand. Again, not really bad things. While nobody would argue that something had to be done to overcome the stiff prejudicial obstacles towards opportunity, much of Affirmative Action's policies skipped right over opportunity and implanted minority students and workers into deep water for which they were not always prepared.

Problem? Nobody said anything about the ability of the minorities who were to be placed in the workforce, or the talent of the minorities to be placed in the classes. Additionally, and this is the greater factor here, since workforces and classes have size limits, which white people would be denied entry because of the new policy? While white resistance helped throw up a roadblock to Affirmative Action, the method of implementing Affirmative Action goals disenfranchised many deserving people of color. For instance, many of the new workers had few if any basic reading and math skills. Same with the new students. Remedial work needed to be done to bring workers up to speed, and tutors were needed to help students over the threshold of higher learning. Did that happen? No. What happened is what is commonly referred to as the 'dumbing down' of society. The bar was lowered, and not just for minorities. Now we buy coffee in cups that say "Caution, coffee is hot" on the side, because we are too stupid to know that. We have cigarette packs that tell us we will die if we smoke them, as if we didn't know that anyway (of course, there are teams of lawyers around the country arguing that some people really didn't know that). Lack of competition removes challenge. Without challenge, at best everything stays the same. At worst, it goes backwards.

Don't believe me? Let me tell you this. There was a man in my law school class who could not read. And, yes, he was black. Oh, he could read signs and menus and things. But he could not possibly have been able to read the application for admission to the college of law, because he could not read cases and make any hay out of them whatsoever. He could not garner a grain of understanding from what he read in any Reporter or casebook, and was eventually held back to the class behind me. I do not know if he ever graduated from law school, but it would not surprise me if he did. This is not to say that there are not people of color who are well-suited and ideally prepared for professional life as doctors, lawyers, professors, you name it. But there are people of all colors, including whites, who are not talented enough or driven enough for professional careers, and being black or another minority doesn't and shouldn't be a determining factor when extending the opportunity to pursue such a career.

You see, we lied to the black population as a color of people and told them they can be anything they want to be in this great country, but we began this journey by lying to the white population, saying the same thing. A birthright of sorts. But we are not equal. In fact, we are darn right unequal! We are shown portraits of the individuals who defied the greatest of odds in pursuit of grand successes as examples, but we don't look inside them; we only see the results of what's inside them and make the conclusion that anything is possible, for any of us. And while that is basically true, it is not so simply because we are Americans, but because we are *competitive* Americans, the best of which overcome the greatest obstacles. What drove them to ignore the statistics and overcome the odds, what parental guidance or lack thereof, what perfectly sequenced events helped them jump the obstacles, we may never know. But we know it wasn't handed to them. We know they faced challenges and competed with those challenges and prevailed.

In a large way, the Law believes itself to be the ultimate referee seeking the goal of compromise but always with deference to equality. We the People are too stupid, or too narrow-minded or small-minded or other-minded to see the big picture. Not the Law. Now, remember, there is no "The Law" without "The Lawyers". We must stipulate here that lawyers are but people (although, as we have seen earlier, people with special inhuman skills), and, as people, are no better than the rest of us. Yes, they've achieved a professional and financial pinnacle. Yes, they've, some of them anyway, have worked hard for what they have. But why would we allow The Law and her lawyers to create such an artificial life for the rest of us?

The answer lies in the inherent inequality of us all. Go back to chapter 1. If we were all equal, we would all be lawyers. Or we would none be lawyers.

Now, the notion of leveling the playing field, like all social matters the law tries to sort out, doesn't end at the legal arena. Once the example has been set by the Law, a tenet trickles down to the people. Remember Newton's laws? Everything flows downward gravitationally. Good, bad, ugly, it all comes from the top. In our case, and in our world, the Law is at the top. Once The Law has rendered a verdict, that verdict, or edict or mandate starts to follow gravity and begins to invade the hearts and minds of the government, the corporations, the small businesses, the educational system and, finally, the people. Ultimately, we begin to act like the law and lawyers. It doesn't help much that television is crammed with "legal" shows and forensics shows that only feed the fire of the amateur lawyers within the world of the viewing public (more later). In the course of a generation or three, we the people have adopted this style of "thinking like a lawyer", whether through necessity or simply trying to appear chic and progressive in a world hell-bent towards inhumanity.

The small businessperson must navigate the tightrope of employment discrimination and premises and product liability. He or she must not only concentrate on how to make a better mousetrap more economically—in fact, that's the easy part—but must spend countless hours and large sums of money dealing with Federal, State and Local compliance, all in the face of an "enlightened" public carrying around the litigation card right in its top pocket.

Employment issues alone are all-consuming. The businessperson has to make darn sure there are no favors being parlayed, even to deserving employees who merit favor, especially if the eyes of the Affirmative Action employees are paying close attention. Remember, employees who have been thrust upon employers under the guise of Affirmative Action only know one way to obtain and keep a job: The Law. The Law has taught them to forget their understanding of fairness and right and wrong; to forget the archaic theme of hard work and paying one's dues; forget work ethic and pride in workmanship. The Law will level your playing field!

Once in the job, the employee who has been hired due to government pressure will continue the crusade, forcing special treatment for race and/or gender specific matters. Maternity leave and child daycare are late-20th century inventions employers have had to deal with since Mom went to work.

(*By the way, the fiction that two incomes are necessary in this day and age is not only ridiculous, it was invented by a few generations of children in adult bodies who still cannot live without their toys*).

A valuable and productive working mom, necessary to the viability of the small business due to her training and experience, takes weeks off the job in order to give birth and spend a few quality moments with her newborn child. The Boss juggles staff (usually requiring unwelcomed overtime for some employees) and "makes do" without his essential employee until she returns to work and things improve. For a while.

Women, for the most part, will not like this next assertion.

Women, for the most part, think with their hearts. Given a decision to make, women will, yes, toss the matter about in their minds for a period of time. But, if the matter in any way involves a woman's emotions, and if those emotions are ignited by the matter, she will, in most occasions, "go with her gut." A decision made that involves a significant amount of emotion is usually not the right decision. I've defended people who've made these "decisions," usually involving alcohol and an automobile or a knife or their fists or a Louisville Slugger, oh, or a Bic lighter and a can of gasoline. "Kill the umpire!" screams an emotional fan. No, important decisions must be reasoned to a rational solution.

Thank God for women and their emotions, especially their maternal emotions. Women were created to be the nurturer of our children, the coddler, the swaddler. Take a woman out of that environment and, while she may be very successful at something else (like multi-tasking, the first skill of any successful mother), her emotions and her primeval nature call out to her to return to the den. But decision-making requires thought, brain thought.

Now wait a minute. Are there highly successful women in leadership roles? Of course. Way more successful than me, for sure. And they got that way because of a disciplined nature that forces them to follow logical thought progression in problem-solving. They fully understand how they are made, and make no effort to hide their femininity or their unique biological place in the history and future of life. They just don't funnel their decision-making process through a myriad of emotions. Sure, everybody, male and female, feels emotional about some topics, some decisions. We'd be inhuman not to. But the best leaders just don't let those emotions make up their mind for them.

A child needs his mother. He or she needs mom to be close during the first several years of his or her life. Mother and child make a connection nine months before the child's emergence into this world, and that connection needs to be nurtured and shaped and fed. A mother who drops her child off at the daycare at the tender age of six weeks does both she and her child a tremendous disservice. Mom can never truly ignore the annoying voice in the depths of her being calling out to her, calling her to duty. And child wanders aimlessly in search of the unique and familiar place of security.

So, our mom returns to the workplace after six weeks with her newborn and picks up where she left off. Both Boss and Mom should be happy. But Mom gets a lot of calls from the daycare and sometimes has to leave in a hurry to attend to a maternal matter. Oh, and let's not forget about the unofficial "breaks" she takes to discuss her new child with co-workers and customers, showing pictures and telling stories, that all leads to a reduction in productivity. That's nothing. Most of her time "on the job" is really just on the outside. Inside, she's thinking about her baby. She can't help it. (And who can blame her? I'm a father, and I'm always talking about my kids at work, while I'm working. Being a barber and owning my own shop gives me great latitude in what I can say and think. However, I talk while I work, because if my productivity slows down, my customers get grumpy and maybe go somewhere else to get their hair cut.)

Enter The Law.

The Law says Mom is a minority, because she is a woman. Forget that half of the people on this planet are women (in Florida, women outnumber men because a man's life expectancy is several years shy of that of women). The Law says these minority women need to have the same workplace opportunities as their male counterparts, and that in order to make the "reasonable accommodations" for new moms, employers should be encouraged to establish daycare centers at the workplace. Now that's cheap, huh? Daycare Centers are the unhappy beneficiaries of almost more regulation than the workplace. Now our employer has had to do without his essential worker for some of her pregnancy, the delivery, and the six weeks after. And, with her mind elsewhere, he's done without her productivity ever since she came back. He's not happy. Now, he has to open a daycare center or, at the very least, adjust Mom's workday to allow her to arrive late and leave early to be within the Daycare provider's schedule. Bye bye small businessman.

You say, Wendell, why can't he just terminate this employee? HA! Don't get me started on that! Terminating an underachieving employee, especially one who has some tenure, some experience and some years of stellar work history, is not that easy in today's litigious society. Labor unions paved the way for a slough of regulations for those working Americans who are not represented by unions. And while it's true that unrepresented American workers have a multitude of rights, the solidarity and legitimacy of the labor union is absent.

Enter the Employment Attorney. He or she has a few tools to level the playing field, which used to be largely in favor of the employer and perhaps rightfully so. The Law saw the benefit of labor unions and found a way to parlay their power to the unrepresented worker by codifying into law some of the major focus areas of the labor movement.

We've already discussed organized labor, but here's a brief summary. At the turn of the twentieth century, the United States was 80-85 percent agrarian, with most Americans making their living off the land. Political and business leaders saw the tide turning in favor of industrialization and lured, little by little, our dads and granddads (and eventually us) from the farm to the city, putting them to work making money building or developing the resources that would constitute the framework of the future: steel, coal, oil, railroads, automobiles. Eager companies with "vision" saw nothing wrong with a guy working 18 hours a day with little or no breaktime, in a horrible, unsafe working environment for a relative pittance. Children too. And what happens if a worker does get injured on the job? Or misses a week with the flu? What about promotions or cross-training? Anyway, you get the point. The field was not just not level, it was so far out of level that people were actually falling off the other side, so something had to be done.

Maybe some guy in the shop or the yard or the plant or the factory went to the boss and asked if the guys could work less or if the company would help out with the medical bills for John's arm, broken by one of the poorly-maintained machines, or if they could maybe get a few minutes break in the morning and a few in the afternoon, to go to the can or to get a drink of water or have a snack or just take a breather or a smoke.

If the boss knew what was coming next, he would have screamed out, "OKAY!!", but he didn't, he said "no," and, "and if you don't like it, you can go back to the farm." Well, to the right the workers saw the insane amounts of money the boss was making, and to the left they saw who was responsible for that income, and they smiled. Without the workforce, they reasoned, the boss would be out of business. Soooooo, they organized, and they bargained. The Boss said, "I can get fifty guys to take your places in an hour," and they workers said, "not if we clobber 'em before they get through the front gate," and the Boss saw that they were serious and he had no choice.

At first, the unions wanted only that which seemed within the bounds of human decency, fewer hours per day, more break time, lunch time, better working conditions, a little financial help when a worker was injured on the job. And no children on the job. Then it evolved into better pay, much better pay, extremely better pay, obscenely better pay, sick leave pay, vacation pay, health care pay, profit sharing pay and, ultimately, retirement pay. Add in job definition and contractual "progressive disciplinary" procedures, and the playing field is artificially tilted against the employer, who is now extorted into a larger-than-necessary, lazy workforce that he simply cannot fire for any reason.

Workers not represented by unions sought out representation. Some got it, some didn't, but that didn't deter them from waging a private war against the very employers who provided them with a way to make a living. But a war needs warriors, and, while many well-meaning people and employees have the guts for battle, they do not have the tools or the knowledge (or the magical key to the door to the legal system, money) to even begin to fight.

So our working mother above, while sitting in front of the tube one evening watching some well-dressed idiot handing out a single, long-stemmed rose to each of the five "finalists" *vying for the opportunity to be his wife*, happens to see a commercial for a large local law firm.

"Have you been injured on the job or through no fault of your own? Or, have you been injured in an automobile accident? Do you feel you are the victim of workplace discrimination? Call the law firm of..." blah, blah, blah. She calls and tells her story and they've heard it a hundred times before. They'll call it a "hostile work environment," in which the boss is asking for only that which he got when he first bargained to hire this worker, that which he is no longer getting from her through no fault of his own, but none of that truth will matter. The Law has him stone cold. If he wants to run his business, he MUST hire minorities. If one of his employees has a baby, he MUST provide reasonable accommodations for her, or suffer an expensive legal battle in which it matters not if he wins: he'll be broke.

All of this because of a notion of fairness that permeates every facet of our society. Everyone is the same, has the same rights, the same privileges, the same opportunities, same same same. And yet, we expend tons of energy establishing our own identity, not only as individuals, but as races and classes and religions and creeds and genders and national origins. We demand to be treated equally in the midst of our battle to remain autonomous.

In the last analysis, all of the Law's efforts to level the playing field would be almost laudable if they were indeed altruistic. But we all know by now that lawyers will never earn a penny without dispute, and that an environment filled with adversaries pays the bills. The greater the adversity, the greater the financial reward to the lawyers who fight the case. Take away the money, you take away the lawyers' motivation. No?

Let me ask you this: How long do you think Alex Rodriguez would play baseball for $50,000 a year?[17]

So who's to blame? After all, that's the question good lawyers ask everyday. By that, they mean "Who, in the grand scheme of this dispute, could be somehow, even tangentially, to blame who also is in possession of large sums of money?" But I ask it here as a pathway to thoughtful introspection, a type of self-examination. Because if lawyers and The Law have taught us to think this way, to be always on the lookout for an opportunity to engage the law in a dispute in which we feel "victimized", then perhaps they are to blame. But where does this notion of finding someone else to blame end? At some point, We The People are compelled to look into the mirror and see if we have handed responsibility for our own actions and our own lives to another—the state, the employer, the federal government—in the fashion that we've been taught to do so.

The news is not all bad. I've met many, many people in the course of my life, both as a lawyer and otherwise, who simply refused to sue—a doctor, the employer, a neighbor, a retailer, a

---

17 By the way, since Mr. Rodriguez has admitted to using steroids, apologized and uttered his unending devotion to the game, wouldn't it be a great testimony for him to go back to the league minimum for a couple of years to prove it?

a car dealer—even though I felt they each had worthy cases. In a way, that's sad. Sad because the message to the potential defendant is that their actions or inaction or other failure is somehow okay. The potential plaintiffs in these cases all felt the same: Somebody made a mistake, and we're all allowed to make a mistake. Okay, I buy that because it's true; every pencil has an eraser.

But some mistakes are made simply because the market has been relieved of the positive impact of competition by a legal system that feels it can cure all ills with money, and a like-minded insurance industry with wads of dough. See, it's the legal system and not the market that portends to keep the doctor's feet to the fire. Healthy competition among colleagues doesn't exist because we eliminated competition long ago because, well, you've read this chapter already.

But the doctor doesn't care; she's well-insured and pays dearly for the privilege of being under-trained or poorly-trained or just so darn greedy that she's overworked to the point of slipping up once in a while. This doctor should get on the floor and kiss the feet of the patient who had the wrong breast removed and yet, refuses to sue. (By the way, if doctors would only have a warranty program, the malpractice bar would be out of a job, and malpractice insurance would be a thing of the past).

Still, The Law keeps trying to level the playing field. Still, it creates artificial monetary awards for losses that are priceless, or, worse yet, worthless. Still, it tries to define Life, when it begins, when it ends. Still, it tries to vindicate the rights of an individual based upon his being a member of a group or class. But no. The Law's efforts have resulted in greater inequality than before, with a space dividing humans from one another that cannot be narrowed with more law, more lawsuits, more dispute, more enemies.

There is no question we were created equal.

We were not, I would argue, created to *be* equal.

MASTICATING THE FIRST AMENDMENT

Congress shall make no law respecting an establishment of religion, or prohibiting the free exercise thereof; or abridging the freedom of speech, or of the press; or the right of the people peaceably to assemble, and to petition the Government for a redress of grievances.[18]

Whew! It's almost like the Framers tried to get the whole kitchen sink in the First Amendment.

Lotta meat on that bone, eh? And yet, simple enough for almost everybody to understand. Let's break it down.

"Congress shall make no law respecting the establishment of religion ..." means we can't have an official religion, and the government cannot pass a law recognizing any one religion over the other. But what about passing a law that directs tax dollars into the coffers of certain "faith-based" organizations? What about providing bus transportation to students of a parochial school? Better yet, what about giving tax dollars to a hospital run by a religion? "...or prohibiting the free exercise thereof..." means the government can't stop us from worshiping in whatever faith. So what happens when the "free exercise thereof" meets "the establishment of religion," like when a high school that receives tax dollars acknowledges, allows and condones daily prayer? And consider the questions surrounding a woman of the Muslim faith, which prevents her from showing her face in public, who wishes to obtain a driver's license in the

18 Amendment I, United States Constitution

United States. Does the Constitution allow her to be photographed with her face covered? You can see where this black and white that we all think The Law should be gets grey.

It was Jefferson himself who, in 1899, said the establishment clause was intended to erect a "wall of separation between church and state." Those words are not in the First Amendment, but those words are often used by secular leaders of our society to continue the persecution of, particularly, Christians. The American Civil Liberties Union often cites these words, again not a part of the First Amendment at all, to prevent children from praying in school (even saying grace prior to a meal), to prevent financial assistance to humanitarian organizations with even the most tenuous religious connection, and to challenge the thousands of references to God within the confines of our government—on government buildings, on currency, in our Pledge of Allegiance. The ACLU is really just a bunch of lawyers, acting like lawyers do, but with a certain axe to grind. Frightened to death of the prospect of life after death, of a Heaven and Hell (and, most likely constantly under siege by the Holy Spirit), these lawyers wage a very public battle against people of faith on every front, and the further people get from a relationship with their Creator, the stronger the ACLU gets.

But how does the ACLU prevent kids from praying in school?

In 1962 (seeing a pattern here with regard to when the whole problem with the Law began to subdivide and conquer?), the Court heard a case regarding New York's law requiring the recitation of a prayer by school children, commonly referred to as the "Regent's Prayer." New York did allow students to refrain from reciting it, or even leave the classroom during the recitation. Of course, the Court held that such behavior was of the type the establishment clause was intended to prevent, and I can agree, to a point. But Congress didn't make a law directing the kids to pray. Congress didn't make a law saying that children have to recite this prayer. Again, the encompassing language of the Fourteenth Amendment requiring equal protection of the law, and the Supremacy clause of Article VI of the U.S. Constitution have worked together and opened a plethora of pathways to the Supreme Court for issues not pertaining to the Federal Government in any way. The large centralized government so thoroughly hated by the Pilgrims and the Framers became a reality through these channels (and, of course, the Commerce clause, discussed later).

So we have a direct challenge on a direct matter dealing explicitly with a governmentally established religious activity. That's the first punch.

Next, the Court heard challenges (1963) to a kindergarten class's required daily selected scripture readings, and ruled that scripture was like prayer, even though the selected scripture readings were chosen for their rather generic moral guidance and literary value. That case came out of Pennsylvania and was called *Abington School District v. Schempp*. What's important about this case is that the Schempps were Unitarians and would later allow that the lawyers in the case convinced them to move forward with the lawsuit, even though the Schempps themselves really had no argument with the requirement.

That's another problem. Lawyers with an axe to grind or a fee to expand, who've been taught to see the ins and outs of all sides of a legal issue, seek to exploit a legal iota even if it means flushing a very good thing for the betterment of society down the toilet. Their attitude is not "well, it's a pretty good idea, so let's see how we can fix this tiny legality," it's "well, this "T" is not crossed and this here "I" is not dotted, so we have to trash the entire idea." I'm reminded of a Gary Larsen "The Far Side" cartoon in which a rescue helicopter pilot has spied an obvious castaway on the beach, bare-chested, waving his arms frantically standing next to rocks arranged to spell the word "HELP!" However, at some time, some of the rocks were inadvertently moved around a bit. The helicopter pilot is speaking into his microphone saying, "Nope, cancel that; I guess it says 'HELF!'" That's exactly what lawyers do. Now anyway. Used to be that lawyers tried to fix things, tried to find ways to get around the itty bitty wrong stuff in order to keep the huge right stuff. Not anymore. Again, the longer a lawyer can keep a case going, the larger the fee is going to be. In an increasingly greedy profit-driven society, more is better, as long as it's money.

The other point raised by the *Schempp* case is how lawyers will use sometimes reluctant plaintiffs in order to get a case worthy of the Supreme Court's eyes. True enough, plaintiffs sometimes grow weary as the wheels of justice grind on. And yes, plaintiffs often need a cheerleader to keep their motors running. But I learned that sometimes, sometimes a lawyer needs to listen to his or her clients, those who no longer see the merits of dragging out the lengthy suit anymore, because clients, unlike lawyers, forgive and forget, and move on.

Next victim? The benediction at high school graduation. How dare, the Court said, the State inflict its religious views upon a gaggle of innocent high school seniors (fraught, of course, with teenaged pregnancy, juvenile crime and widespread drug and alcohol use), at "one of life's most significant occasions," commencement. In 2000, a case out of New Mexico held that a prayer prior to a high school football game was in violation of the establishment clause. Funny, how many times have you seen this scenario: A professional football player lies motionless on the field after a violent block or tackle. Immediately, the vast majority of the players from both teams form a circle, drop to a knee, bow their heads and close their eyes in fervent prayer for their colleague's benefit.

The Law is waging a very real war against The People, and it's winning via the systematic unraveling of a society knit from the yarn of faith. Okay, okay, we don't want the government establishing a state religion or supporting one religion or no religion over another. I can accept that. What in the world does that have to do with the right of the majority, the vast majority, of people exercising their brand of religion, no matter where they happen to be? Again we are extolling the virtues of a tenet that holds that a tiny minority of people should get not just equal time, but more than equal. A few people don't want prayer in school, so now nobody gets to have prayer in school? What kind of a republic is that? That's not a republic, that's a dictatorship, rubber-stamped by the government. In fact, in all likelihood, what the government is really doing is violating the next clause of the First Amendment, i.e. prohibiting the free-expression of religion.

Keep praying, folks.

The Freedom of Speech. Many people think of the freedom of speech whenever we talk about the First Amendment. A lot of people think we have an unabridged freedom of speech, because the First Amendment guarantees it. But you know The Law, it just can't leave well enough alone. In the case of abridging the freedom of speech, the ends justify the means.

Time? Just after the beginning of the First World War. In a truly free society, one should be able to speak freely with regard to his government, to gather together with like-minded individuals, even if it means they are plotting to overthrow that government. That's freedom's essence. But, The Law said, in order to maintain the integrity of the union (to wit, to prevent another catastrophic Civil War), the government has the right to thwart seditious and "treasonous" speech. War is a tough time for a republic, especially in a relatively transparent republic, one in which people have a bevy of rights. Not everyone, it seems, supports war. And although it's quite obvious that the majority of Americans supported our efforts in both World Wars, there were those who vocalized their opposition.

Congress' first attempt to circumvent the First Amendment, ostensibly for the protection of the United States' security interests, came about in the Espionage Act of 1917. The Espionage Act of 1917 was a United States federal law passed shortly after entering World War I, on June 15, 1917, which made it a crime for a person:

to convey information with intent to interfere with the operation or success of the armed forces of the United States or to promote the success of its enemies

to convey false reports or false statements with intent to interfere with the operation or success of the military or naval forces of the United States or to promote the success of its enemies and whoever when the United States is at war, to cause or attempt to cause insubordination, disloyalty, mutiny, refusal of duty, in the military or naval forces of the United States, or to willfully obstruct the recruiting or enlistment service of the United States.

In the handful of cases to come before the Supreme Court, all the defendants who had been charged with violating the Espionage Act had their convictions affirmed. In the case of *Schenck v. United States*, Justice Oliver Wendell Holmes (and no, I wasn't named after him) asked whether the actions of American Socialist Party secretary Schenck—distributing 15,000 leaflets to young men, encouraging them to avoid the draft—presented a "clear and present danger" to United States security of the type Congress sought to prevent. (You may have read Tom Clancy's novel or seen the movie Clear and Present Danger. In that story, the President of The United States used Justice Holmes' phrase as a threshold to an executive order with regard to the Columbian drug cartel. That's a different story).

Obviously, Justice Holmes' phrase (which, if we remember from earlier about how Judges and Justices operate, is a glimpse into the particular leanings of Mr. Holmes) failed to convince the majority of the court, and perhaps because it wasn't issued strongly enough. In a later case, Justice Holmes took off the gloves and clarified his stance in a dissenting opinion in *Gitlow v New York*. He (joined by Justice Brandeis) said that the government must show that the speech (in this case, the *Left Wing Manifesto*) presents a "real and immediate danger". Sounds suspiciously semantical to me. But that's how lawyers work. You may argue that there is little, if any, substantial difference between the two phrases. Lawyers don't care what you think.

By the way, it was in the *Schenck* case that Justice Holmes stated, unequivocally, that the "most stringent protection of free speech would not protect a man in falsely shouting fire in a theatre and causing a panic." People like to quote the "fire in a crowded theater" line when they propose placing limits on free speech, but Holmes attempt at analogy is a red herring, for the First Amendment is only about placing limits on *Congress*.

Lots of cases came before the Court in an effort to interpret the "clear and present danger" language. Depending upon the makeup of the Court and the facts and language of the various statutes that were being challenged, the Court really never did define exactly what speech could be so egregious as to be proscribed, and courts across America find themselves—on the heels of 9/11 and the security measures taken by the Federal Government—trying to determine what speech fails the test.

As you may have guessed, the Government's answer—remember, enforced through the Law—is less free speech. I read a story just last week about a man in Mobile or Memphis (I forget which) who was arrested after publishing a statement indicating that he'd like to assassinate President Obama. Amazing, isn't it, that a television full of talking heads can usurp the boundaries of common decency and decorum and spew lie after hate-filled lie about "Bush" or some other hated politician for whom they refuse to use the proper title, and a guy with a computer can't utter his feelings without violating the Law?

Hate speech is another of those areas where lawyers and judges disagree. Again, where does the line between just speech and speech intended to arouse action fall? Not long ago, we saw a popular morning radio host lose his job because of a racial slur (only to win the job back, with a raise, after the lawyers clarified the terms of his contract). Isn't it true that, like beauty, hate speech would have to be in the (ear) of the beholder? What's that say about people? Thin skinned? Defensive? Ready to fight at the drop of a hat? Amazingly, the ACLU's position on so called "hate speech" is simply this: It doesn't exist. Say anything you want, says the ACLU, let the marketplace of ideas sort it out. Here is the same problem JFK and his progeny isolated when they publically segregated the races, the genders and the "differently able": Once you make that distinction, once you call attention to the difference—and clearly establish one as inferior and thereby inferring there exists a potential for discrimination—the problem only escalates.

Why, for instance, is the "N" word hate speech, but so many of the slang terms for nearly every ethnicity and race around the world are not? The word "bitch" ignites rage in one woman and inspires pride in another. Is it hate speech for the one and not the other? I really don't know. But I do know that much of what has evolved as so-called "hate speech" is a product of the Law. Why? Come on, haven't you been reading?

The major point to remember in all of these cases is that they represent a chipping away of what I see as clear and stalwart Constitutional mandates by Congress via the Law. How equivocal is the statement "Congress shall make no law... abridging the freedom of speech"? Of course, lawyers and the courts and The Supreme Court back into these First Amendment cases through language contained in other areas of the Constitution having to do with protecting the union and such. But it's not as though this is the Thirtieth Amendment. So Congress does make a law, one it knows may have Constitutional problems, the President signs it—everybody here is on board, for the protection of the Union—and it becomes law. Then the lawyers get hold of it and the cases begin to come up and then the Supreme Court gets to sort it all out.

I wrote a paper in my Constitutional Law class for law school about so-called 'advisory opinions.' The Supreme Court does not issue 'advisory opinions' on pending legislation, because Article III of the Constitution spells out that the Court will hear only actual "cases and controversies." I made the argument that it'd be nice if the Court would render advisory opinions on proposed legislation before it becomes law. My Con Law professor thought it was great, and I now know that he did so because he wasn't a litigator. How'd it be for the profession if all the finer points and potential rocky areas of a proposed law were neatly ironed out during the lawmaking process? Where's the money in that?

Fighting Words are a lot like hate speech, but they are not necessarily aimed at any one of the multitude of protected classes of people under Title VII. Fighting words are defined as speech so egregious and inflammatory so as to most likely illicit a violent response. Again, remember that in the Law we bounce every idea against the fictional "Reasonable Person" to see how it stacks up. But even the reasonable person has to admit that the list of potential fighting words has to be pretty long. You add in non-verbal speech and the list grows. Look what could happen. One driver cuts another driver off in traffic. The one driver gestures with that internationally recognizable symbol, extending his middle finger (this action is best accompanied by a sneer or some other nasty facial expression, as well as a string of incomprehensible epithets). Driver two exits his car with a tire iron, taking exception to the gesture and/or the poor driving. Driver one gets his skull cracked in while claiming 'freedom of speech', and Driver two says 'nope: Fighting Words'. No matter what, lawyers are involved, adding fuel to the fires of dispute.

One area of speech that is just getting out of hand lately is in the world of Advertising. I know, I said I wasn't going to visit this topic, but advertising is another of those monsters that reaches out and touches each of our lives almost constantly, that it's important for you to know how much Law and how little truth is involved in the process of enticing you to purchase a good or service.

Remember when you were a little kid, watching cartoons on Saturday morning? You thought you were enjoying the antics of Bugs Bunny and the Road Runner, Scooby Doo and Johnny Quest, but really the only reason for this entertainment was what happened between the shows. You already know this, I understand. But the conditioning by advertisers at those tender ages set us up for a lifetime. We watched television commercials for all sorts of toys that we just had to have. We weren't gifted with the critical thinking skills to see the deceit lying just under the surface. Advertisers showed little girls playing with a roomful of dolls and their clothes and cars and houses that doubled as carrying cases—a wonderful make-believe world of endless enjoyment—then lightly tossed in the disclaimer: Dolls and accessories each sold separately. (It was the same with boys' dolls, too, only boys don't play with dolls so advertisers went with euphemism: Action Figures.)

Before the widespread availability of home radios, and long before the epidemic of television, advertising was mostly contained in print, newspapers and dailies who's focus was actually on the news. Businesses realized that their message could be delivered en masse to every household in the community via the local fish wrapper and customers came. When first radio, and then television took off, advertisers realized that they could not only get the message out through these mass media outlets, but could tailor the broadcasting of their message by sponsoring dramatic and comedic entertainment that would surely keep the attention of listeners and viewers long enough to make their individual case for biscuits, motor oil and the local car dealer. The truth is, without advertising, there would be no television shows.

In the beginning, advertising was simple: Buy Our Product. But as competition between rival gas stations and laundry soap companies increased, the advertising message had to be refined such that consumers chose one brand over another. Television advertising evolved into scientific psychological warfare rife with outrageous claims and empty promises. Left alone, the Market would have winnowed out the scurrilous fakes and consumers would have had the final say-so about which products lived up to their claims and which were useless. But companies began to receive complaints. Products did *not* live up to the claims made in their advertisements. Washing machines broke down. Cake mixes didn't rise. Paint didn't cover, not like the commercial said it would.

At first, companies made amends. It was easy, after all, because the boost in sales due to the advertising provided windfalls to companies; a few disgruntled customers were easily appeased with replacements and refunds. But competition in the marketplace became fierce, and the unrealistic claims became legendary. (*I actually believed that P.F. Flyers would make me "run faster and jump higher"*). Companies grew, sales volumes went through the roof, and the growing numbers of disgruntled customers were not so easily hushed. "There oughta be a law," they said.

And The Law said: "Cool."

The Law, it felt, should protect its subjects from the onslaught of these hi-tech roadside hawkers. Congress created the Federal Trade Commission to, ostensibly, regulate trade practices and oversee advertising. But really, as with so many federal regulatory agencies, it seems their real job is to conflagrate life with an endless supply of convoluted legalese. After sixty years of "regulation" we find ourselves worse off than if we'd left the whole thing alone.

Show of hands: How many readers can even see, let alone *read*, let alone *understand* that tiny block of letters at the bottom of a full-page automobile ad? How about that quick flash of what has to be words at the bottom of the television screen? You know, the one advertisers zap up there right when the scantily-dressed model gives you that look as she's slithering into the passenger's side and her short skirt rides up a bit? How about this: You're driving along with the radio on and a car ad comes on promising whatever—50 miles to the gallon, ten year "bumper to bumper" warranty, "zero" per-cent financing—and then, in the last three seconds of the ad, the Fastest Talker In

The World sets the record 'straight'? All of this is the Law talking, and it's called "Disclaimers." Think about it. Advertisers are allowed to say just about whatever they want, and we've been conditioned from a young age to disbelieve (remember the "talking dolls" you couldn't understand, the 300 piece model airplane with "some assembly required", and, alas, the sneakers in which you ran no faster or jumped no higher?). But we're an optimistic bunch, we Americans, and we still think we ought to get the truth from advertisers. So the Law jumps in. After all, if commercials told the truth, we'd never buy their products...or would we?

I suppose the pharmaceutical industry has to be one of the most successful businesses out there. In a country involved in a decades-long war on drugs, Americans consume more drugs by far than anybody else in the world. Not too many years ago, drug manufacturers, hotly competing for dollars provided mostly by Medicare and other insurance, recognized the potential for advertising and went after consumers with astonishing results. Astonishing because—and kudos to the FDA for finding the regulatory strength in the face of a powerful lobby—the advertisements were required to fully disclose any potential side-effects.

Now nobody is a stranger to the barrage of pharmaceutical advertisements that consume the time between your favorite shows each day and night. Watch them closely, and you'll see that the actual pitch for the drug lasts about 25 percent of the time, while the list of potential side-effects consumes the balance. Why anybody in his or her right mind would take a drug to, say, lower cholesterol, that can increase the chances of having a stroke or heart attack, or cause liver disease, or cause (gasp) sexual side-effects is beyond me. Of course, a physician is quite prepared for these potential problems, and is more than willing (given the vast amount of "non-monetary incentives" from the pharmaceutical industry to do so) to prescribe a drug to counter these side-effects.

Over 40 percent of Americans are on some kind of prescription drug, and, according to the Florida Medical Examiners Commission, prescription drugs kill 300 percent more people than illegal narcotics.[19] We Americans are heavily medicated (forget about alcohol and tobacco), and we hunger for more, to the point that we entirely disregard warnings predicting fatal side-effects in a pathetic act of misguided optimism. We take drugs for everything from cancer and heart disease to weight loss and, especially, to overcome age and our bad habits that cause diminished sexual drive and performance. And yet we demand to be prescribed them and we buy them and we complain about their high cost, but oh, we want our drugs.

But by and large, prescription drugs are toxins and poisons that doctors provide us with to placate the symptoms of our disease or illness. Yes, there are painkillers that numb us when we are in pain, and so narcotic are they that thousands of patients emerge from pain treatment as hopeless addicts. But there is no drug on the market today designed to heal your illness or vanquish your disease. Not one. In fact, many multiple drug-users are taking a drug whose sole purpose is to counter the side-effects of another drug. True.

We crave poisonous substances rather than healthy behavioral modification to counteract the effects of stress and depression. Why? Because it's easier to do so. Americans have become creatures who feel we are entitled to a life of leisure, a life that plants our overweight bodies in front of the television set, where we endure the onslaught of misleading and tantaliz-

---

19 *Natural News*, November 10, 2008

ing advertisements that promise us more leisure and, when that catches up to us, drugs to kill the pain and numb the mind.

So drug advertisers give you the full disclosure, and not even quickly spoken or written in tiny letters, and yet we buy, we ingest, and we escape. Okay, so I digressed some here, but only because I honestly believe that we as a society are medicating ourselves right out of the dialogue, and right into the place where the law wants us to be: weak-minded, weak-willed, emotionally over reactive and, ultimately, victims of our own undoing.

And, when you've gone overboard, when your own actions have taken you to a place with drastic consequences, you remember the advertisement for that lawyer, that distinguished member of the bar who will find somebody else to blame for your own bad decisions, all without you lifting a finger, or spending a penny.

In 1977, a case out of Arizona called *Bates v. State Bar of Arizona* changed forever the practice of law. Generally speaking, that case held that prohibitions on lawyer advertising were a violation of the First Amendment. The ensuing thirty years have reduced what was once an upstanding and revered profession to a gaggle of carnival hawkers, replete with empty promises to "fight for your rights" and, of course, to get you a large amount of unearned income. As I noted earlier, the competition is so stiff amongst the huge saturation of practitioners that lawyers have become very creative in "discovering" new and uncharted areas of "negligence" and clients to exploit them, and then use the mass media advertising venue to build a stable of clients. Tobacco litigation alone garnered billions of unearned dollars for clients, and, of course, lawyers. I even heard of one case in which the law firm, realizing that the defendant tobacco company's appeals would consume ten or more years (and their client would surely be dead by then), petitioned the court to get their 30 million dollar fee up front!

Tobacco litigation spawned more outrageous lawsuits: fat people sued fast food, diabetics sued Big Soda, bankrupt gambling addicts sued casinos, and DUI victims sued the bars that served their negligent drunk driver booze. Amazingly enough, many of these irresponsible plaintiffs won!

Lawyers reached out on all fronts, but the Personal Injury/ Wrongful Death/Medical Malpractice Bar has to be the most egregious. These areas of the law epitomize the long-held business tenet that it takes money to make money. Wealthy law firms utilize their buying power to take good cases against big insurance companies on a contingency basis. A client with a good case, one like we talked about earlier where the case law is so thoroughly established that winning is almost guaranteed, needs only to sign the contingency contract. In contemporary times, this contract usually binds the client to being financially liable for any and all out of pocket expenses of the law firm, and something in the neighborhood of 30-40 per cent of the ultimate award for a fee.

Well, that's all well and good if a law firm wins millions for a client. 60-70 per cent of $10 Million is a good chunk of change, but that kind of award is usually set aside for those injury victims who are and will never be in a position to benefit from it. Usually paralyzed—but often deceased—these Plaintiffs' lives are forever changed by the negligence of another, and no amount of money will ever get them back to normal.

But what about the Plaintiff who hires a law firm on a contingency who wins $100 thousand? This award amount usually stems from a vehicular accident in which the Plaintiff was injured, maybe even permanently, although not noticeably, if you know what I mean. Take the $15-20K for costs away, and that leaves $80K. Now, the lawyer gets his 40% *of the total award* and that leaves $40K for our victim and, statistics say, that'll be gone within 12 months.

My favorite thing about these Lawyers' advertising is how they tell you how they will fight for you, all the while situated with a backdrop of a courtroom or a court house. Let me tell you this: These cases will never see the inside of a courtroom. These cases will settle outside of court, often without you even being involved. Both sides will go through the motions of preparing for a trial: taking depositions, accumulating evidence, getting independent medical exams, whatever. The ruse is in place so that everybody in the chain of events has an opportunity to get his or her slice of the pie. And once the entire matter is prepared for court, and all the reams of paperwork have been filed, the Plaintiff's lawyer and a lawyer for the insurance carrier have a conversation on the telephone and negotiate a settlement.

It's just the same as our Eminent Domain matter earlier in the book. Everybody gets paid but the victim never gets his or her day in court. Of course, the Plaintiff can always reject a settlement offer and go to court but there are two things going on here. First, anything can happen in court, *anything*. A really good case can meet the wrong jury and you can lose. It happens. The other thing is that it's already been maybe two years since the accident that caused this litigation you're in. A for sure settlement looks a lot better than more time and the possibility of getting nothing.

Insurance companies and doctors and hospitals have historically been adverse to defending themselves against claims by injured victims, simply because the cost of so doing usually far exceeds a meager settlement amount. That and, as we've said earlier, the cost in bad publicity is often great as well.

Competition in the Personal Injury/Wrongful Death cases is getting so out of hand that lawyers are using the benefit of 20/20 hindsight in order to persecute well-intentioned manufacturers of long ago. Does it seem fair to you that a product deemed safe and beneficial forty years ago that now appears to have been the cause of illness and death of a certain amount of people should *now* be a gateway to huge monetary awards? The only possible way in which these Asbestos cases could have any chance of winning is if a) the manufacturers *knew* it was unhealthy and b) withheld that information from those involved in using it. Oh, yeah, there's another way: Grab On To The Coattails of Tobacco Litigation.

Which is what happened.

Nobody's saying that asbestos is a great product, and nobody's saying the dust created by asbestos is safe. Not now. But back then, back then when we were using it because it was a fantastic insulation and sound barrier, back then when it had value in the construction of hundreds of thousands of applications from schools to municipal buildings to ships, nobody knew it was unsafe. People got sick, couldn't breathe, died.

And that's sad and that's history. Unscrupulous lawyers hauling these manufacturers and builders and contractors into court forty and fifty years after the fact is not only unethical and immoral, its blatant goal of lining the pockets of greedy lawyers is transparent.

The case against false and misleading and downright unethical advertising as a basic freedom of speech issue will never be resolved. It is really up to consumers and passive viewers to create in themselves a vigilant filter, one that thinks critically and asks the common sense questions. My father used to say that a good business doesn't need to advertise, and I think of that whenever I see any business killing itself advertising its products and services.

And, in general, I don't believe anything I see on the television.

When it comes to the Freedom of The Press, the only area that really fits into this book is the one where lawyers become talking heads. Bill O'Reilly does not practice law, but his status as a lawyer is an attempt to lend credence to his position as an "expert" in many areas, and viewers are led to believe that his show is about truth and justice. Fact is, his loud angry talk is entirely designed for its entertainment value and certainly not its truth value. I find *The O'Reilly Factor* entertaining, and only real "pinheads" (one of his favorite terms) would be hypnotized into believing that the show is meant to be anything but.

The other, more dangerous person who fits this category is Nancy Grace. Famous for rendering "Guilty" verdicts without benefit of evidence, testimony or any other Constitutional guarantee, Ms. Grace relies upon feminine (and now maternal) emotion to work the tide of public opinion against a person arrested for, usually, a heinous crime. Forget "innocent until proven guilty." Nancy Grace wants to move right from the booking desk to the gallows.

You're saying, "Wendell, isn't this book all about the crap the law has made of us? And, didn't you say something earlier about the lengthy appeals process?" Yes, yes I did. But I've also been talking about a balancing act, and certainly a law that more closely follows that of the Framer's intentions. That means that the "court of public opinion"—which is nothing more than a hi-tech Star Chamber—while having its say, should not be the final judge and/or jury. In the case of Nancy Grace, she is *not* a journalist by trade. She is a former prosecutor who is using the power of the media to sway the minds of the public—already predisposed to its own simple justice. I say it's a Star Chamber not because suspects in a crime are forced to come on her show and divulge all, but because their reluctance to make an appearance on her show allows Grace to fly to all sorts of conclusions and scathing insinuations, taking her audience right along with her. *If you have nothing to hide why are you avoiding me?*

In the last year, Grace has done show after show about the missing toddler, now found and know to have been murdered, Caylee Anthony. Long before her mother was even charged with a crime, Grace was on her case, practically accusing her on television, in front of millions of viewers (okay, really flattering her here) of killing her child. Grace did this based upon the mother's behavior after the child's disappearance and her seemingly conflicting stories given to investigators. But hammering away at this case *every day for eight months?* That's the kind of behavior which, if exhibited by one of my former criminal clients, would have resulted in a psych exam order. True. But again, the problem isn't one of legalities or even ethics. It's one of credibility versus entertainment. A lot of people give Nancy Grace a lot of respect because of her position as a former lawyer. But that was then. Now she's just another entertainer, so remember that when you watch.

There are other lawyers who have become talking heads, and you know them. You know their politics by their network, and you'd like to believe that they actually care. Hear this now: They Do Not Care. They are entertainers who do not even realize their level of self-absorption, and cannot comprehend the life-walk of another human being. Yes, they can *appear* to be emotionally moved. Sure, they can even actually *be* moved, for the moments the camera is rolling. But the truth is that even though the story they are covering is about another, these talking heads think it's about them since the lights and camera are aimed in their direction. For most of them, take away the TelePrompTer and they are hopelessly lost. No heart, no soul. Only an angry, loud-talking actor.

(*And what's the common denominator in all of these shows? Regardless of which side of the political spectrum they lean towards, they all must, at some point in the "dialogue" say something like "Okay, I've got to take a break here, thanks for coming on the show…" In other words, they are compelled to take the time out for the only reason there even is a show: The Commercials.*)

The First Amendment has endured the test of time, but that is the best one can say about it. Its clarity and sharp edges have been smoothed out, overlooked, and especially, disregarded. Who is better to determine the Framers' intent than the Framers themselves? We have volumes of correspondence between the various Founding Fathers regarding their thought processes for the bulk of the Bill of Rights, yet Justices throughout the ages, while sometimes alluding to and even quoting the Framers, instead fall back upon their own interpretations of the actual words on the page. Then we have modern-day Justices building upon the precedent set by the earlier Justice and, before you know it, the intentions of the actual authors of the documents are reduced to the status of myth.

My father used to irritate me when he would build up the sides of our utility trailer and load the thing way high up so as to get the most out of the dump fee. That's what I'm reminded of when I think of the way the First Amendment has been so thoroughly abused. It's as if all the lawyers and judges and Justices are consciously trying to load it up well beyond its inherent capacity instead of just letting it carry the load for which it was designed.

Yes, it's language is quite encompassing, and its reach broad. But it has no language regarding privacy, nor does it have any language regarding a separation of church and state, no language regarding actions that should be protected as speech and certainly no language regarding what kind of speech it intended to exempt (largely, I'd argue, *because it never intended to*).

But the First Amendment is so germane to what makes the United States the unique republic it is: a wide open no holds barred marketplace of ideas and debate, regardless of the injured egos, ruptured esteems or hurt feelings. Had it remained in its place of purity, perhaps so much of the angst infiltrating society would be mere annoyance, and words really would never hurt us.

Defending The "Guilty"

When people find out I used to be a criminal defense attorney, they always ask me the same question: *How can you defend somebody you know is guilty? I could never do that....* I'll spend a couple of minutes attempting to show you the Framer's logic of the Sixth Amendment, and then you be the judge.

Okay, back to the Star Chamber. The Star Chamber was a place, an actual place in King George's London where those miscreants accused of a crime were brought and, under the well-established understanding that confession was 'good for the soul', were *encouraged* to rat themselves out. Proceedings where held in secret, with no indictments, no juries, no witnesses and no appeals. The various forms of *encouragement* included beating, threatening greater bodily harm, and the creative use of fire. Psychologically, it was the equivalent of that scene from an old Western movie:

Suspected Horse Thief: "Sheriff, I'm entitled to a fair trial."

Sheriff: "Oh, we're gonna give you a trial, son. Followed by a first class hangin'"

So, under the authoritative gaze of the collective members of the Chamber, most commoners were convinced to confess, often to crimes they hadn't even committed, in the hopes of minimizing the punishment. Today, cops do the same thing, and will continue to hammer away at a suspect indefinitely, until and unless he or she utters the magic words: "I want a lawyer."

The Sixth Amendment to the Constitution sets forth the rights of those accused of crime:

In all criminal prosecutions, the accused shall enjoy the right to a speedy and public trial, by an impartial jury of the State and district wherein the crime shall have been committed, which district shall have been previously ascertained by law, and to be informed of the nature and cause of the accusation; to be confronted with the witnesses against him; to have compulsory process for obtaining witnesses in his favor, and to have the Assistance of Counsel for his defence.[20]

Like I said earlier, I can only remember one innocent person in my time in the Public Defender's office. That means that there were lots of people who came through my office, represented by a legal-sized file folder (for many, these folders were thick, indeed), whose career path wandered away from the accepted norms of society and into the criminal world. So, yeah, I defended people who I knew were guilty. Back then, I suppose I was like any other of the guys in my office. I felt like "the Man" was doing a number on the poor and downtrodden. I felt like these people I defended were unable to make good decisions for their lives. And I felt like they were laden with one addiction or another, over which, as I saw it then, they had no control. Also, I never asked them.

My view has changed.

They are the ones who did it to me.

Because, of all the people these defendants could have lied to, in the end the only one they actually *did* lie to was me. Isn't that special?

It was always the same. I'd go to the jail on Monday morning with a list of clients who, one by one staggered into the examination room, took a seat across from me and, after a few

---

20 Amendment VI, United States Constitution

niceties, I'd take the top off a pen and poise myself over a yellow legal pad and ask only this question: "What happened?" The client would then avert his or her eyes away from me and begin a story that always ended with the client in the best possible legal light. I remember one story:

"Well, this girl I didn't know picked me up and I got in the passenger's side of her car and we drive around the corner and then the cops come up behind us and turn on their lights and she crams this fake ID and this bag of dope under my seat and the cops come up and ask us what we're doing and we say 'nuthin' and they ask can they search the car and we stall 'em and then say 'okay' and when they find the ID and the dope under my seat they arrest me. But I didn't really know the girl and it was her dope and fake ID."

Then, this client met my eyes again, to see if I, in any way, just bought that story. I don't care. I simply ask the next question: "What did you tell the police?"

"Oh, well, I told 'em that the dope and ID were mine, cuz I didn't want her to get in any trouble."

"And," I continue, "you did this for a woman you never even met?"

"Yep."

Point is, most of my clients already gave themselves up to the police, making admissions that no lawyer could ever get them out of. Why? I'll tell you why. Because their judgment is usually impaired by one or more substances and the police, God love 'em, always tell these suspects that they cannot possibly "help" them unless these suspects get straight with them and tell the truth. Unbelievable.

Let me tell you something right now. The Police have several jobs to do. They provide an important service that often puts them in serious danger for nothing remotely resembling adequate pay. However, *none of the duties they have includes "helping" a suspect of a crime.* Like many other legal public servants, they have sacks full of cases they need to close, and nearly any method of so doing is at their disposal. They will try anything.

In 1963, Ernesto Miranda was arrested for stealing $8. Charged with armed robbery, Miranda was in police custody when he signed a confession for the robbery—and also for the rape and kidnapping of a woman 11 days earlier. Miranda's lawyers appealed on the grounds that Miranda did not know he didn't have to incriminate himself. Of course, the United States Supreme Court overturned his conviction, and that led to what we all know to be the practice of reading an arrestee his or her "Miranda Rights." (The ironic part of *Miranda* is that Miranda was re-tried and convicted upon the proffering of additional evidence. He served time and was released, only to be killed in a bar fight by an attacker who, upon his arrest, invoked his right to remain silent.)[21]

But in today's society, rife with stories of atrocities against children committed by an ever burgeoning cadre of sociopathic deviants, the so-called "Christian Burial Speech" case has to be mentioned. In this case, a police officer utilized some alone time with the suspect to discuss a matter of principle associated with the case.

Mr. Williams was arrested in Davenport, Iowa, for the murder of a ten year old girl who was killed in Des Moines, Iowa, about 170 miles away. Williams, on several occasions, invoked his right to remain silent. During the drive from Davenport to Des Moines in the police cruiser, one of the officers who knew that Williams was a former mental patient and a devoutly religious man said this:

---

21 *Miranda v. Arizona, 383 U.S. 436 (1966)*

"I want to give you something to think about while we're traveling down the road. . . They are predicting several inches of snow for tonight, and I feel that you yourself are the only person that knows where this little girl's body is, that you yourself have only been there once, and if you get a snow on top of it you yourself may be unable to find it... the parents of this little girl should be entitled to a Christian burial for the little girl who was snatched away from them on Christmas Eve and murdered."[22]

Williams led the officers to the burial site and was subsequently convicted of the murder. The Iowa Supreme Court upheld the verdict, but the U.S. Court of Appeals and, ultimately, the U.S. Supreme Court, overturned the verdict, although the Court was split 5-4.

So now you get to hear what I think.

I think about the Sixth Amendment as I thought about the Fourth Amendment. That is, I think the Sixth Amendment was intended to provide innocent people the right to have a lawyer present to do the work of making sure that the interrogator did not use lies and deceit of the type typically utilized in the Star Chamber to convict an innocent person of a crime. I do not think the Framers intended to allow clever lawyers the opportunity to usurp or rationalize or re-define the Amendment so as to allow a person culpable of a crime to go free. I'm not the only one who thinks this way. Justice White, in his dissent, said virtually (*yes, yes, hate that word*) the same thing.

But the truly scary thing about this case—not to mention hundreds of others—is that the Law of the Land, arrived at after countless hours of debate and re-writes by intelligent, educated men, and Ratified by the People of the then Thirteen Colonies, was overturned by one person. One Lawyer. One lawyer with a political agenda, appointed to the Supreme Court for a term

---

22 *Brewer v Williams 430 U.S. 387, 1977*

that could conceivably last until the day of his death. And folks, that overturned Law isn't just a law, it's a *Constitutional Amendment*. And it doesn't just affect one case, but *all* cases to come after it. What if it's wrong? Doesn't matter, it can never, ever be fixed. You cannot un-ring a bell

Listen to me. Five people could change the world as we know it. Five Justices on the Supreme Court could all agree that Miranda Rulings are just not necessary anymore, and they would be gone. Five Justices could decide that your right to keep and bear arms is hinged upon any of a thousand factors like your status as a deadbeat dad or an alcoholic or a bad credit risk and your gun could be taken away. Don't believe me? Hey *seven* people decided that you do *not* have the right to life, re-member? Five people decided you cannot pray in school. Five people decided the 2000 Presidential Election. It all comes down to Five.

The defense of a person known by the lawyer to be culpable ("guilty" is a term for the courts and juries) is one of those areas of the law that laymen often don't understand, because it often doesn't come out the way it's supposed to. Should be that the lawyer stands up and gives her best defense of the charges against the accused and (if the accused is indeed guilty) the prosecutor's case is just better and justice wins the day, right? I mean, a lawyer who knows his client is good for the crime can't argue in court that the client didn't perpetrate the alleged crime, that's not allowed. Sure, she can offer other theories of the crime, and yes, she can offer evidence that may shed some "reasonable doubt" on the case, but she cannot, if she knows otherwise, argue that her client is not the perpetrator. To do so would be grounds for a mistrial, or a new trial if the case was over.

So what do lawyers do? Well, like me, they just don't ask if their client did this thing he or she has been accused of; only ask, "What happened?", and the client will supply the rest. For the clients who do tell the truth, the logical pathway is often the "Plea Bargain."

Plea Bargaining is a twentieth-century invention used by the courts to speed up the process of the criminal law. As we've seen, prosecutors and public defenders are really just administrators of the criminal courts, moving truckloads of cases through the judicial system at breakneck speed in an endless drive towards expediency. Plea Bargains are also less-expensive than a full-blown trial, requiring only a modicum of effort at investigation from either side and the assurances of a convincing advocate to steer the client into the probation office.

Plea bargains, in and of themselves, are not bad things. In fact, many criminal defendants have emerged from the process much better off than if they'd gone to trial. Some have emerged waaaaayyyyy better off, a fact often angering victims and their families. This outcome often happens in rape cases when physical evidence has been destroyed and the reputation of the victim might not be as agreeable to a conviction as a prosecutor would like. Victims often feel doubly violated; first by the perpetrator and then by the Law.

But plea bargains, often due to their economy, can and do also lead to a criminal defendant feeling pressured into pleading to a crime for which he or she is not culpable, simply to forego a criminal trial in which the outcome may very well be much more severe.

I'll never be able to tell you for certain that "Sarah"[23] did not do the things the prosecutor said she did, but I've always had my doubts. I'll never be able to tell you because the public

---

23 Not her real name.

defender's office hadn't the money and Sarah hadn't the time or money to wait out a lengthy investigation while her child was in the custody of protective services.

Sarah was a 27 year old hard-working single mother whose husband had gone on a business trip to Oklahoma one day and never returned. Their son, Christopher[24] was five at the time. Not long after, the local police came to Christopher's kindergarten class armed with anatomically-correct dolls and asked questions in front of the entire class, including the teacher.

"Does your mommy or daddy ever touch you here?" they asked, and pointed to personal areas on the dolls.

Christopher raised his hand. "My mommy touches me there every night," is what he said. He didn't see anything wrong with that.

Representatives from child protective services and the prosecutors' office, as well as a police officer trained to investigate crimes against children took Christopher to a private room where they asked more questions, without anybody present who could remotely be called an ally to Christopher. He eagerly answered these questions, one of which was, "when does mommy touch you?" The answer? "When I'm in the bathtub."

Five people in the room never even connected the dots on that one, because they were pre-disposed in a terrorist-style media-driven atmosphere of child-protection to smoke out parents who were abusing their kids. See, in a jurisdiction two hours away, police discovered that a set of six-year-old twin girls had been repeatedly sexually abused by their parents since they were two, a disturbing case that prompted the type of investigation that led me to Sarah and Christopher. (Police did the same thing during the seventies with marijuana. "Does

---

24 Again, not his real name.

your mommy or daddy have a little pipe like this at home? Or how about this tall glass pipe? Does your daddy roll his own cigarettes?" that kind of thing.)

Our own psychologist met with Christopher, and so did I. He was happy. He was healthy, and he was outgoing and cheerful, all of which behavior flew in the face of the accepted symptoms of a child undergoing abuse at home. During our own questioning, Christopher told us his "pee-pee got ticklish" when his Mom bathed him at night, and that it sometimes "got straight out". I did some cursory investigation and found that many boys do become aroused at touch before puberty and, given that evidence and his good spirits and lack of any symptoms of an abused child, I felt we had a pretty good case. All we'd need is a decent expert to testify about Christopher's all around well-being and I felt we could provide reasonable doubt. Alas, we could not afford a decent expert.

When I first met Sarah at the jail though, my first doubt set in. She was a tall, well-groomed woman who had no obvious signs of any drug or alcohol addiction. She presented herself as one who understood the charges, however, even though she looked me in the eye as we spoke and even though she seemed eager to assist in her defense, her demeanor was too casual, and, I remember writing in my notes that she never asked me how her son was doing. That bothered me, even though I had already told her I'd been to see Christopher and he was doing well. A mother in such a situation should be crazy to be separated from her son, and she didn't seem like she was. When she said, "*I don't feel like* I've done anything wrong," my heart sank. My gut told me she was lying. If she had said, "I haven't done anything wrong," I'd have felt better. But she didn't. Trouble was, I still didn't think she was a child-molester, based upon my meeting with Christopher.

As a lawyer, I knew one thing: This woman would hang herself on the stand, so I could never put her up there. Trouble is that, even though a defendant in a criminal trial is under no obligation to take the stand in her own defense, her failure to do so can send a fatal message to the jury, regardless of the judge's instructions to the contrary.

(Quick note about Judge's instructions. When a judge gives an instruction to the jury to disregard something they've just heard, that instruction serves only to underscore and highlight that thing they just heard. I rarely asked a judge for such an instruction. So when a judge tells a jury that the fact that the accused did not take the stand in her own defense should not be used as any evidence of guilt or innocence, juries usually feel like something is being hidden from them.)

The prosecutor had decided to charge Sarah with six counts of felony sexual assault on a child under the age of 12, and five counts of reckless endangerment of a child. I thought that, at most, they could maybe convict her of one of the felony counts. Problem is that one count could send her to prison for almost the rest of her life. I don't think my pal the prosecutor wanted to do that, and I know he didn't think she deserved that, but that's how the criminal law works its way to the plea bargain. Sarah had found bail money and was sitting in my office the next time we talked.

"What should I do?" she asked me from across the desk. I had asked myself a thousand times before that day the same question. She was dressed in a conservative beige dress that dropped almost to her knee, a low heel and not much makeup. She sat there not uncomfortably, but not totally comfortably either. I still had my serious doubts about her ability to sway a jury with her equivocation on the most important of questions.

"Sarah," I began, "anything can happen at trial. We have a pretty good case, but not great…" I left out my feelings regarding her as a witness. "I don't think you're a child molester, but only you know that for sure." I went on to explain that the prosecutor was offering ten years' probation on a plea to the child endangerment charges, and that it would mean regular visits by Child Protective Services. I waited for her to say something like "I just want my son and I to go home and be a family together again…" but she never did. It always bothered me.

Sarah was smart enough to see that she had no choice. That pickle didn't seem to drive her crazy like it had so many other clients who just felt powerless against truthless "facts." Because the choice between life in prison and ten years of probation is not a choice, especially not for a single mother who loves her kindergartener. But the Law doesn't care about that. And, believe me, I understand that police need wide latitude with tactics in the modern day in order to counter a sophisticated criminal element that includes a creative criminal bar. But police have to do credible investigations aimed at finding the truth and must change the focus of their investigation when it becomes apparent that their hunches are not supported by the evidence. In Sarah's case, the media-induced hype that terrorized a region by raising questions in people's minds regarding parents' behavior put pressure on the prosecutor and the police to make darn sure that, if they had anybody like that in this jurisdiction, he or she was going to pay for it.

I felt powerless in this case, too. There were times I just wanted to stand up and yell at Sarah, "Dammit, are you sexually abusing your son or not?" but I didn't want to find out the horrible truth, if there was one, because then I couldn't ever argue that she didn't do it, not in court anyway. The last time

I saw her was at her plea hearing, where she answered the questions the judge asked, never admitting guilt but taking the deal because it "was in her best interest" to do so. She slipped her purse over her shoulder, shook my hand and thanked me, glad it was over. I wanted more than anything for her to be completely innocent, but I'll never know for sure.[25]

So, you be the judge. Could you have defended Sarah under the circumstances I've just outlined? Do you think she deserved a defense? Was Sarah guilty?

My real problem in this case was that I cared. I cared a lot about that little boy. If I were in private practice and Sarah came to me with wads of cash and handed me her life to defend, what would I have done? Well, I would have fought feverishly, gotten second and third opinions, hired a stable of experts and argued that the prosecution was on a witch hunt. I never would have put her on the stand and I'd have won that case which would be great if Sarah was innocent, but not so much if she was not.

Why did I tell you this story? Because it illustrates how the lawyer's job is infinitely easier when he hangs his emotions on a hook and just advocates. But, as we've seen, that is the kind of step lawyers take towards an unstable existence devoid of conviction and absent truth, whose sole reward is money. Which is a large part of the reason people hate the Law and her lawyers.

---

25 If anybody wants to shed light on this, email me at daddysflying@tampabay.rr.com

Manufacturers' Never-Ending Liability

One of the greatest benefits of operating an old-fashioned barbershop in south Florida is that I have a pretty good handle on the price of every good and service for the first half of the twentieth century. That, and the weather "up north" during January, February and March. My customers supply this information to me on a daily basis:

"My first haircut cost a quarter," is how it begins.

Then another will say, "Shoot, when I was a kid, you could get a whole bag of groceries for two dollars."

"My daddy earned $24 *a week*, and he was a truck driver."

"I remember gas at about twenty-three cents a gallon."

"A pack of cigarettes was 16 cents."

"My first new car was a '43 Plymouth that cost me $710 dollars, including tax."

You get the point. We have a lot of fun reminiscing around here.

But, I *do* remember when you could buy a lawnmower, a regular push type Briggs & Stratton, for about $25.00, down at the local Western Auto. Now, I'm sure that inflation has had an impact on the price of lawnmowers, but there came a time when there was a significant jump in the cost of a new lawnmower, thanks to an emerging area of the law called "Products Liability."

Who on Earth is incapable of appreciating the danger associated with sharpened blades spinning at a thousand RPM?

A lawnmower is not a dangerous instrumentality in the legal sense, but it is a very dangerous machine, capable of inflicting serious injury and dismemberment and even death, especially if it used improperly. Which, according to the products liability bar, is how you will use it because you are too stupid to know otherwise.

Products Liability is another of those areas of the law designed to protect us from, well, us. Why does somebody feel we need such protection? Go back a couple of chapters; 40 per cent of us are on prescription medication. The rest of us are impaired by something: alcohol, over-the-counter cold remedies, illegal drugs, television, the Internet, you name it. The operation of machinery, including motor vehicles, is generally discouraged while under the influence of Nyquil, let alone alcohol and illegal drugs. Yet, that is exactly what happens every day of the work week in the United States. Workers traipse off to mundane jobs to operate dangerous machines while under the influence of one or more mind and body impairing substances.

Years ago, I worked for a mid-Atlantic utility company for a few years. The satellite office I worked in employed about 200 people; everybody from secretaries and management to job engineers, linemen, fork lift operators and truck drivers. Of these 200 people I'd estimate conservatively that 150 were regular marijuana users. By that I mean at least weekly; many, *many* were daily users. Oh, and you know that big orange Igloo cooler you see on the side of these utility trucks? That was used as a big beer cooler. First stop in the morning was the local Seven Eleven to fill the Igloo with as much beer as it could hold, along with its already legal cargo of ice and water. I'm not kidding.

So, off to work we go. And the machines we work with are dangerous. They are supposed to cut things off and pound things flat and drill holes and press things together, and for those tasks they have spinning blades and heavy presses and sharp drills. And safety protection. And employees to perform regular maintenance on these machines. Man and machine working together is a beautiful thing; until somebody gets hurt.

I don't know what the first products liability case involving a worker and a machine was, but I'm positive that case led to the installation of protective safety features, which increased the cost of the machine, and additional liability insurance for the machine's manufacturer, which also increased the cost of the machine. See, when an employee is injured on the job, the employers' Worker's Compensation coverage handles the cost of the injury, as well as lost time wages, etc. (More on Worker's Compensation later). There are even coverages for lost limbs, eyes, permanent injuries and death. But, frankly, until recently it wasn't much.

When an employee is injured on the job by a malfunctioning machine, all the legal eyes turn towards the manufacturer of that machine because—anyone? anyone? That's *right*—that's where the money is! Yeah, but you say, "Wendell, what about if the machine was made and sold a long time ago and the manufacturer hasn't even seen it in seven years and for the last seven years hasn't it been somebody's job in the company to maintain that machine and shouldn't somebody there be responsible?" Short answer? Nope. Once you make a product and send it into the "stream of commerce" you have essentially issued a warranty that that product is fit for a particular purpose in perpetuity.

So, here's our scenario. Guy comes in on Monday morning, hung over, still drunk or, worse yet, under the influence of one of a myriad of drugs, legal or otherwise, maybe still half-asleep, probably not at all delighted to be back at the job he totally hates, and he fires up his shelf-sawing machine. And, he's out of it so he sets it on "Automatic," which means that at regular time intervals, without him having to do anything, the saw blades, like a hungry Osprey, will quickly descend upon a length of lumber and angrily hack them into usable lengths. Now, over the past few days, he's noticed that one of the blade areas keeps getting bunged up with sawdust and shavings. He's mentioned it to the boss, but is content to, during the blades' up stroke (and on "Manual") simply wave his hand at the area and brush this debris away. Today, though, he's a little slow and the machine is on "Automatic" and well, you know how this ends.

Okay, you've been reading, so I'll ask you: What's the next question? *Right!* Who's to blame? And remember, by that we mean 'who is tangentially attached to this scenario who is also in possession of deep pockets?' Because our boy with the missing arm is going to get his Worker's Compensation (used to be called "Work*man's* Compensation"), which is the agreed-upon amount for the loss of a limb and perhaps for re-training in a field requiring only one hand, etc. But that's going to amount to, *maybe*, $25,000. Now, we've got the boss and his maintenance staff's blunder, but this is a small cabinet shop and there's just not that much there, either.

But the manufacturer is a huge German conglomerate and all one has to prove is that it "knew or should have known" about the potential for the machine to clog up and the potential for injury and the case is over before it began. Now the award is $1 million. But that's the *total* award, so let's break that down by first taking a look at something called "Comparative Negligence."

Comparative Negligence is the modern method (that is, the "money making method") of apportioning blame in any tort action (we haven't said yet, but a Tort is just a fancy name given to any number of things that one person or entity can do to another, usually out of negligence but also intentionally). Time was when the Common Law had a doctrine called "Contributory Negligence," that is where a Plaintiff in a case, if found to have contributed to his injury in any way, literally had no case. In other words, if a person was jaywalking and you hit him with your car, you could claim contributory negligence and it was a complete defense against the claim. It was beautifully simple and it kept people on their toes. Under such an umbrella, if our lady who spilled coffee on her lap was found to have contributed to her injury in any way, she gets nothing. Contributory negligence kept people personally responsible for their actions that contributed to their injury, like when my son goes running through the house and catches his ribcage on the corner of our big heavy dining room table and goes down in a pile of yelling and tears. He gets nothing but sympathy under the doctrine of Contributory Negligence: He shouldn't have been running. But, as we have seen, there ain't no money in that.

Today, Comparative Negligence is the method used by the courts to apportion liability for any given case. Typically, it is used in automobile accidents in which there are at least two vehicles and two or more potential causes. Let's say you're driving along 15 mph over the posted limit and a motorcycle comes blowing through a stop sign right into your path and you cannot stop. The "but for" test means that if you were not speeding and if he did not blow the stop sign, the accident would not have occurred. But it did and now the court has to apportion liability, finding you 40 per cent liable because of your excessive speed and the motorcycle driver 60 per cent liable because of his failure to stop at the stop sign. Let's say the jury awards $200,000. Well, our motorcycle driver gets only $120,000 as a result. (And remember, his lawyer gets at least 30 per cent of the *total award* plus expenses, so we're down to about $50K, and a new Harley costs at least $20,000, so you see how the whole thing winnows down).

Comparative Negligence is further broken down into categories: "Pure" Comparative Negligence means just that, like our example above. The blame is apportioned and the award adjusted to accommodate for the percentage of contributory negligence of the Plaintiff. There are two types of "modified" Comparative Negligence. In the first, if the Plaintiff is deemed to be "at least" 50 per cent culpable, he gets no award. In the second, if the Plaintiff is deemed to be *more at fault than the defendant(s)* he gets nothing. Only a few jurisdictions still use modified Comparative Negligence and, as you might have guessed, in those jurisdictions, televisions don't light up with a river of personal injury lawyer advertising at all hours of the day and night.

So, we're back to our angry, bitter, impaired amputee. Take his million dollars and subtract the fee, maybe as much as $333,000, and costs of litigation, perhaps as much as $100,000. Now, run that award through the Comparative Fault grinder and maybe the jury decides our boy is 30 per cent to blame, maybe more. Anyway, subtract 30 per cent from that million and you get $700,000. Take away the fees and costs and you get $267,000. For your *hand*.

Now, you say, Wendell, how come the lawyer's cut didn't come just out of what the guy got after the Comparative Fault math was done? Come on, you have to ask? Because the contingency fee contract doesn't read like that, silly; the fee is based upon the "total award," regardless of how it ends up being apportioned. You didn't read that part of the contract, did you?

Now, granted, $267,000 sounds like a lot of money, and sure, it isn't chump change. But when it's gone—and statistics say it will be in just over two years—it's gone and so is your hand.

But it doesn't end there.

Let's say the manufacturer adds safety devices designed to protect our dimwit from himself. And let's say that this safety device works well, but cuts production by a third. And so, let's say the company boss tells his maintenance people to override the safety device, and let's just say that our dimwit knows the safety device has been overridden. In that case, you'd assume, the manufacturer couldn't possibly be held liable, right?

Wrong! Our creative personal injury lawyer will argue that the manufacturer, in its infinite wisdom (and enjoying the profit from its machine), should have *known* that the safety device would cut production which would have logically resulted in an end user overriding the safety device and so it should have engineered and installed a "backup" or "fail-safe" safety device and that argument works because, after all, the manufacturer is a deep pocket.

By the way, can you imagine a jury deciding that a company who puts this kind of machine into the stream of commerce should have to have that kind of foresight? That would take a skilled lawyer indeed to put the black hat on this manufacturer such that the jury members would see it as an evil empire whose sole goal is to make money.

Few jury members think, "Hey, that company could be mine," because people who own successful businesses and companies *get out of jury duty.* Chew on that a minute. Lawyers don't want intelligent, conservative people on juries, because they tend to see things logically and through the use of a lot of common sense. Common sense has no place in the courtroom. Lawyers (in civil trials anyway) want people on juries who think with their hearts, whose malleable emotions lie just under the surface, just waiting to be manipulated.

The cases against machine manufacturers by workers injured on the job have kept thousands of lawyers busy for entire careers. And you see what happens: Precedent. One case leads to another and another until the precedent in place is that a manufacturer is held liable for its machine nearly forever. Sure, Comparative Negligence often discounts awards, but the precedent is set forever. Unless one end-user were to modify a milling machine to work like a catapult, the manufacturer will almost always be liable for any injury it causes.

And the costs associated with the liability, the retrofitting, the retro-engineering, everything, gets passed along to the point that the bulk of the cost of an item to the end user (like the shelving unit or the cabinet made by our dimwit's employer) is not in materials or workmanship, but in regulation and the Law. It is just another way in which the Law invades our private lives. You say that we've brought this on ourselves, that our own stupidity (or impairment) has led to the increase in product liability litigation and increased costs associated with that litigation. Yes, but which came first? The need for protection from ourselves or the lawyer who saw a potential prey and capitalized upon it? What if, say, we kept Contributory Negligence? What if any contributing fault of our own acted as a complete defense to the plaintiff's allegations of negligence? My theory is that people would be more careful. People would take their time to do tasks safely or pay the consequences. And, people who were found to be 100 per cent non-contributory would win lawsuits. How beautiful is that? You'd have about half as many lawyers, maybe even less.

It all goes back to the premise of this entire book. The Law has chosen to arbitrarily and with little invitation paint our lives with a broad brush, filled with as much Law as it can muster, and certainly more than we'll ever need. The Law is like a terrorist, using a single event to put a strangle-hold on all other events forever. Nobody would argue that there have been serious injuries caused to people through the negligence of another or others; the casebooks are full of them. There *should* be lawyers to fight for the rights of people who are victimized as a result of the carelessness of another or others.

But accidents are just that, accidents. Mistakes. The presence of an eraser on the end of every pencil is evidence that we all make mistakes. Pointing out the mistake of another is both educational and neighborly. Dragging somebody into court because he or she has made a mistake, and demanding that he or she go bankrupt in order to make you "whole" (and then some) would never have become commonplace without lawyers. But, like I said in the introduction to this book, the media makes sure we hear about the atrocities, and we all become afraid. Get the lawyers involved, and we all become greedy.

Remember the Ford Pinto? Great little car, sporty but gas-sipping. Lots of people had Pintos. Then, in May of 1972, a Pinto in which Lily Gray and a 13 year-old acquaintance were traveling was struck in the rear-end, igniting the gas tank and killing Ms. Gray. A jury that heard the case awarded a total of about $3 million in damages, but astonishingly awarded $125 million in *punitive* damages. The jury heard evidence regarding two things: First, that a safer design of the gas cap/gas filler pipe was scuttled by designers at Ford and Second, because of the reason the design was scuttled: money.

Designers, working with employees of Ford in the Cost/ Benefit Analysis department (the so-called "bean counters"), decided that the design would cost approximately $11 per vehicle, and would save some 180 lives. Ford, crunching the numbers, decided that the total cost of litigating the cases of the additional 180 dead people (at least the ones Ford believed would sue) was less than the retro-fit, and decided against it. That really did not sit well with the jury. Tossing lives about as nothing more than numbers and profit will do that.

Let's take an aside to discuss Damages. There are basically two types of damages in a civil case: Compensatory and Punitive. Compensatory damages are those quantifiable monetary amounts a jury awards a victorious plaintiff in order to make the plaintiff "whole," or as near whole as can be achieved. (Obviously, if a plaintiff is missing body parts that cannot be replaced or is forever imprisoned in a wheelchair by the adjudicated negligence of the defendant, "whole" really means something else altogether). If, as is sometimes the case, the negligence in question rises to the level of "recklessness" or if the injury is caused by intentional action by the defendant, a jury will often award Punitive Damages.

Punitive Damages are an interesting component in private lawsuits. The history of punitive damages is debatable, and the wide variety of holdings regarding valuation of punitive damages evidences no established formula for arriving at punitive damages. However, Judge Posner (a well-known Federal Appeals Court judge and a prolific writer)[26] *did* say that punitive

---

26 Lawyers even argue over the correct pronunciation of Judge Posner's name: Long "o" or short "o". Honestly.

damages are not a function of the identity of the defendant but of the degree of recklessness or intent.[27] Yeah, right. You really think the jury didn't consider the fact that it was the Ford Motor Company being sued here?

Some argue that since the compensatory damage amounts might be insufficient to make the plaintiff whole (after subtracting legal fees, costs, etc), punitive damages are a way to get the full amount of compensatory damages to the plaintiff while the rest of the money goes to pay the lawyers. Either way, our lawyers are getting paid. And very well, at that.

By the way, who decided that the punitive damages should go to the plaintiff? Why can't they simply go into a fund overseen by the court to compensate individual victims who come out of the woodwork at a later date? That way, the victim could be made whole and there would be no need for another round of expensive and protracted litigation...oh, right, that *is* the reason.

And what about Class Action lawsuits? Ever get a contrived letter in the mail from a law firm thousands of miles away indicating you might be part of a class of potential plaintiffs in a lawsuit against some entity? The paperwork, usually several pages of legal mumbo-jumbo in about a 5-Font, basically tells you that the case has really already been adjudicated or settled and you may be entitled to relief. Read on.

What it usually says is that, if you agree to be a part of the class, and the settlement is "approved by the court" your potential windfall is usually no more than a few bucks. "But, Wendell," you say, "it says right here that the suit has been settled for $150 million, and there are potentially 1 million plaintiffs. The math doesn't work out right." Right. That's $3 million to the plaintiff class, and $147 million to...*anyone?, anyone?*

---

27 *Mathias v. ACCOR Economy Lodging,* 347 F. 3rd, 673, 676

Okay, so we've got a handle on "damages"; not to be confused with "injuries," damages is money.

Now, automobile safety issues go back a ways. In 1965, Ralph Nader published his now famous *Unsafe At Any Speed*, detailing what he saw as both design flaws in the Chevrolet Corvair as well as insinuating that design engineers for Chevrolet—as well as the other big three makers—were not as concerned with vehicle safety as they were appearance and styling. Nader argued that the suspension and suggested tire information were insufficient to prevent the wheels from caving under the vehicle in turns at speeds greater than 30 MPH. While criticism of the findings in the book were challenged by GM, it was not until unbiased engineering tests were performed that Nader's "conclusions" were found to be more hype than factual.[28] Moreover, by the time Nader's book came out in mid-1965, Chevrolet had already recognized and corrected the problem in the new models.

But the damage was done. The lawsuits rolled in and regulatory agencies were birthed and, even though the auto industry was already at work on methods and equipment to make automobiles safer, they were now under a deadline to bring them on line. Head rests, energy-absorbing steering wheels, shatter-resistant windshields, and safety belts. *(And then there were CAFE standards, and then there were UAW contracts only a lawyer could love, and then there was stiff competition from the Far East, and then there were bailouts paid for by you and me and, by the time this book sees the printing press, there may be no more General Motors Corporation. Thank you very much, respected members of the bar).*

---

28 PB 211-015: Evaluation of the 1960-1963 Corvair Handling and Stability. National Technical Information Service. July 1972.

While the Corvair issue was questionable, the Pinto debacle caused Americans to face a fact: Corporations just might not care about you as much as they say they do in their advertisements. Add to that the Watergate scandal, and the level of mistrust in the hearts and minds of Americans was off the charts. Now, with nothing sacred and everything a potential for litigation, in stepped the lawyers.

Establishing themselves as the only thing separating the people from the dreaded corporation/government/insurance company, lawyers found their stride, and they've never looked back. But their hunger for money and their thirst for blood outlived their usefulness, and, as the corporations both a)improved their products and service according to market pressure, and b)hired their own stable of barrister bulldogs, lawyers just found other areas of the Law to exploit, and other fears to instill in the litigation-ripe populace already evidencing a disinclination towards personal responsibility.

Aspirin is a great pain reliever. But, since it is a drug and, as such, a poison, it has side effects, not the least of which is the damage it can do to the lining of the stomach. So, scientists scurried about for a pain reliever that didn't contain aspirin, and the result was Acetaminophen, marketed as Tylenol. (Few people know that the active ingredient in Tylenol is responsible for the deaths of approximately 16,000 people each year).[29] But it wasn't the active ingredient that killed 7 people in the Chicago area in 1982. It was Potassium Cyanide, injected into individual tablets by a lunatic who has never been identified. Nevertheless, that single act of terrorism led to what we all struggle with each time we need to gain access to one of a myriad of over-the-counter medications: The packaging.

29 What You Don't Know About Tylenol Can Kill You, Dr. W. Gifford Jones, Canada Free Press, September 8, 2003

The FDA's response to the Tylenol murders was about the same as the Federal Government's reaction to the 9/11 World Trade Center tragedy. Now every single package of over-the-counter medication is equipped with safety sealed packaging, supposedly to prevent the kind of tampering that killed those people in 1982. Never mind that that same FDA *approved* these drugs, drugs that kill people everyday. Anyway, it is just another example of crisis intervention in America, and product liability law designed to protect us from ourselves.

Look around. A 15-year-old boy is killed on an ATV, a "four-wheeler", and immediately the Law steps in with regulations requiring training, helmets, safety equipment, automatic shutoffs, speed-squelching governors, you name it. Pretty soon, it's not even fun to ride one anymore.

My point is that nothing is 100 per cent safe. Once you make the conscious decision to use a machine or take a drug (or vice versa), you have to undertake some personal responsibility for that thing. But, over the years, the Law has said we don't have to assume any responsibility. "Do what you want," it said, "and we'll straighten out the mess." So now, when we screw up, when we have a mental lapse or make a bad choice and get hurt in doing so, we don't worry about tomorrow; the nice-looking chaps on the television promising to make everything alright and "fight for your rights" will ride in like a knight in shining armor. Again, maybe we do deserve the law we get.

Now, back to our lawnmowers. I was about 12 years old when my father was taken to the emergency room with his second heart attack. While there, the paramedics brought in an old man with one of his hands wrapped up in a blood-soaked towel. His daughter told us that he'd had a habit of tilting his lawnmower up on its side while the blades were still turning and then rinsing the blades with the hose. (And what would

Drew Carey say?). Well, the old-timer lost his balance and fell into the spinning blades and not then and not there, but somewhere else, a lawyer got wind of a similar situation and went on a rampage against the lawnmower manufacturer and the Consumer Product Safety Commission came on board and now there are spring-loaded handles that kill the engine if you take your hand off the mower handle and that costs money and that adds to the cost of liability. Does it surprise you to learn that there are over 400 law firms in the United States who hold themselves out as "experts" in lawnmower accident law?[30] No wonder that simple little push mower costs over $200.

---

30 My Definition of "Expert": "X" is an unknown value, and a "spurt" is a drip under pressure.

The Second Amendment:
The People's Last Defense

"A well regulated Militia, being necessary to the security of a free State, the right of the people to keep and bear Arms, shall not be infringed."[31]

Of course, the Bill of Rights would have no teeth at all if it weren't for the Second Amendment, which gave The People the right to keep and bear arms. What good is the right to petition the government with grievances, to have the right to keep the various checks on the Federal Government without the means to physically overthrow that government if it got too big for its britches? I mean, the new Republic was formed as the direct result of a rebellion against an oppressive force, and that formation came about because a group of farmers, shopkeepers, blacksmiths and writers put their money where their mouths were: they got their guns and they used them. Some have opined that "The Second Amendment was written to protect The First Amendment."

Second Amendment litigation has historically been based upon the so-called "Framers' intention." Two schools of thought have emerged, based, interestingly enough, on the grammatical construction of the Amendment itself. One group of interpreters believes the first clause regarding the "well-regulated militia" was intentionally written as a framework for the right to bear

---

31 Amendment II, United States Constitution

arms. That is, the *individual* right to bear arms hinged upon the *collective* and temporal or occasional need for a "militia." The second group understood the first clause to be a "non-exclusive" reason for the Amendment itself. In other words, the right to bear arms as individuals was the given, one reason for which was if there emerged a need for a "militia."

Now, that all seems like semantics and, as we have seen, lawyers live for semantics, but the courts have consistently come down on the side of the right for The People to own and carry firearms. Some state statutes, however, as well as federal statutes, have placed limits upon both of those rights.

As recently as 2007, the District of Columbia had a law on the books prohibiting the ownership of certain weapons, especially handguns. *The Firearms Control Regulation Act of 1975* banned residents of D.C. from owning handguns, automatic firearms and certain high-capacity semi-automatic firearms.[32] In 2008, the United States Supreme Court ruled that the Act was an unconstitutional violation of the Second Amendment.[33]

Forty-Eight States allow the carrying of concealed weapons, although they all require a process of application and permitting in order to do so. Many pro-gun activists believe that the Federal Government, under current Democratic control, will seek to restrict both gun and ammunition ownership, as well as the carrying of concealed weapons.[34] Attorney General Holder is on the record as saying that the *Heller* opinion has no basis on the various Anti-gun statutes in the other states, and has

---

32 Enacted September 24, 1976.
33 *District of Columbia v. Heller, 554 U.S. ____ (2008)*
34 White House Chief of Staff Rahm Emanuel, Attorney General Eric Holder, and Secretary of State Hillary Clinton are considered to be the strongest Anti-Gun voices within the Democratic Party.

steadfastly maintained that the Second Amendment does not protect an individual right to bear arms.[35]

But, what difference does it make to the big picture? I mean, if we view the rationale of the Second Amendment as a means for the People to keep a check upon the Federal Government, how can such a check be realistically achieved when the People have small arms and the government has highly sophisticated weapons and weapons systems at its beck and call? Even if we The People could afford them who's going to sell us tanks? Fighter jets? Artillery? In the interest of national defense, we've allowed our elected officials the right to vote for huge spending of our tax dollars on weapons that you and I simply could not acquire. Once we did that, we essentially gave up our right to bear arms, for the originally intended use anyway.

It's no secret that firearms are used everyday by some people in the commission of crime. The Law has outdone itself in efforts to curb these illegal uses of firearms and, in so doing, continues to silently lobby the People out of their Constitutionally-guaranteed right to keep and bear them. If you've been victimized by one of these low-life's, it's understandable that you would demand some kind of restriction on guns. Truth is, however, that no amount of legislation or regulation would ever keep guns out of the hands of those who would use them to do harm. This fact is just further evidence that an oppressive centralized government that arrives at its own legitimacy through the use of The Law achieves its only effectiveness against law-abiding citizens.

---

35 From *Amicus Brief* in *District of Columbia v. Heller,* 554 U.S. _____ *(2008).* An *Amicus Brief* is written by "distinguished" lawyers and legal scholars in support of one side or another in cases that go to the Supreme Court.

Googling the phrase "Gun Law" results in almost 17,000,000 hits. The seriously vast amount of litigation, regulation, legislation and legal commentary on firearms law is sobering. The simple directive of the language of the Second Amendment, like everything else in The Law, seemingly cannot be left alone. Political and social realities dealing with the noxious presence of gun-related crime in the United States foster a never-ending debate over the ownership, use and carrying of weapons by the People. Lawyers love it.

My reason for bringing up this topic now is really two-fold. First, and certainly foremost, is the fact that in the first few weeks of 2009 the United States Government has exhibited a blatant disregard for the will of the People, to the extent of voting for historic spending legislation, ostensibly to stabilize the nation's economy. Huge amounts of the People's tax money are being handed over to America's largest banks and the U.S. automakers General Motors and Chrysler in an unconstitutional and unprecedented act of transfer of wealth such as that found in Socialistic governments of whom the U.S. has always been critical.

Picture this: George Washington approaches Congress and asks for a million dollars to help out one of the early banks. Can you imagine the backlash?

America is ripe for Revolt. The People are speaking alright. Telephone logs during the Senate debate over bailout money to the banking industry indicate a ratio of 100:1 against any such use of taxpayer money. They passed it anyway. The same objections were highly voiced regarding the bailout of the auto industry.

In the barbershop, the comments are nearly unanimously against such action.

"If I were to run my business into the ground," said one customer, "who's gonna bail me out?"

"If I can't manage my company right, and it goes belly-up, that's the breaks," said another.

And the same is true of my own business. If I price myself out of business, or if I *spend* myself into bankruptcy, oh, well. I lose my business. To most Americans, It doesn't make sense that we should have to use our money to reward companies who exercise poor judgment and drive their companies into the ground, especially when those companies seem to be rewarding their highest-level management with windfall-type bonuses.

But the lawyers in Congress are smarter than we are, I guess. They know things that we don't, because they've been lawyers so long. Remember, they're the 'best and the brightest' of us, elected via a barrage of lies and broken promises and whose sole agenda is to protect their own way of life and get re-elected, no matter how many lives they have to destroy in order to do so.

These lawyers, many of them anyway, have made a career out of a public service job that was supposed to be a privilege, a low-paying or volunteer temporary opportunity to serve the People. They continue to be re-elected despite the fact that they have engaged in conduct unbecoming of the office; many have committed crimes, several have been poor stewards of their own money, some have refused to battle their own lust and other addictions. These men and women are in charge of creating and enacting the law (and spending our money) that you and I are subjected to each and every day of our lives.

The atmosphere is identical to when the United States came into being. Huge oppressive government trying to disarm the citizenry, enacting huge spending programs and compelling The People to pay for them. If the Crown had been successful at disarming us, we wouldn't be a Nation today.

In 1992, FBI agents raided the home of Randy Weaver in Ruby Ridge, Idaho, claiming he was the mastermind of a militia being organized to attempt an overthrow of the U.S. Government. Weaver was alleged to have a cache of weapons and a network of sympathetic co-conspirators. Agents of the FBI and the ATF staked out his residence off and on for several months. On the day of the raid, ostensibly to execute a warrant for Weaver on the charge of missing a court date, agents killed Weaver's wife and 14-year-old son, Samuel, and wounded Weaver. Whether Weaver was forming a militia at that time or not, the sympathy his cause gained as a result of the attack on him by his own government has resulted in the growth of the militia movement in America.

Now, let's clear something up right now. Many Americans believe that, since we have a standing Army and complex military, the reference to the "militia" contained in the Second Amendment is now obsolete. Wrong! Remember that we have two entities here: The Government and The People. The Constitution gave the People the rights contained in the Bill of Rights, and those rights are a direct and intentional constriction on Governmental powers. We've been lead to believe that the U.S. Army is *our* militia, when, in actuality the various state National Guard brigades are better defined as "militia." The Guard, comprised of people within the state, stands ready to be called into duty to defend and protect the People (even if that means defending against an attack by the U.S. Army). That's what Federalism means; the States have a certain sovereignty that, while deferring to the federal government's supremacy, still cherish the will of the People and check the power of that supreme Federal Government, lest it abuse that power.

There exist, however, non-sanctioned and well-organized Militia throughout the United States. Regardless of your personal opinion of these men and women, they see themselves as the last bastion of protection from an uncaring and untruthful Government, a Government that continually thwarts their purpose.

On April 19, 1993, a compound in Waco, Texas housing 81 members of the Branch-Davidian sect were summarily executed by agents of the ATF. These peaceable people were only trying to establish their own society with their own value system, one that emerged as a revolt to what they viewed as an oppressive and secular United States.

Worse than these tragedies are the government-engineered public relations attacks against separatists, identical to the attacks made by the British government against the brave men who one day would be called "Patriots."

Still, constitutional interpreters continue to reaffirm the right to keep and bear arms. Interestingly enough, however, the reason for the right has shifted from one of keeping a check on the government to one of protecting ourselves from our fellow citizens, and for recreational purposes. See, once again the law and her lack of truth has us lashing out at one another, violently seeking the justice her lawyers continue to argue away.

True enough, the Law allows for the non-violent overthrow of the government through the use of the vote. However, the courts have provided legal methods which have been engineered to produce election results favorable to the incumbent. I'm talking about a practice historically referred to as "gerrymandering."

Gerrymandering derives its name from a combination of the last name of Elbridge Gerry, the governor of Massachusetts from 1810-1812 and the word "salamander," since that is what voting districts looked like after this type of redistricting. Gerry was responsible for signing a bill into law that effectively redistricted the voting districts so as to impact the election in his favor of his party.

In addition to forced districting, many people believe that the 2000 Presidential Election was decided by a combination of the Florida Supreme Court and the United States Supreme Court upholding highly questionable voting laws.

In either case, and the second reason for including this discussion in this book, the Law and her lawyers are at the forefront of such illogical and unreasonable and irrational conclusions. And they continue to care less, so long as they get paid (using some of that money to buy handguns to carry for protection). We may never re-instill the once soft-pillow confidence and trust Americans have in their country and their government. But the likelihood of ever regaining that trust seems ever more distant as the Law continues to exponentially expand and tighten its grip on the People. Nevertheless, always remember the old mantra: The Second Amendment protects the First.

Who's To Blame?

So, now we have to ask the big question, the same question lawyers always ask: Who's to blame?

In our litigation-happy society that sees a tidal wave of Law from virtually (*I know, I know, I* hate *that word*) all corners of American Society, who's to blame? In this book, I've tried to show you what I believe, what I've come to glean after some years of law practice and many more years of just observing. I'm convinced that lawyers—even some well-meaning attorneys—judges, justices and legislators at all levels are the major culprits here. Seizing every opportunity to make hay where even no grass will grow—that is, creating a legal case and a lawsuit and a new law nearly out of whole cloth—lawyers, whose sole aim in nearly every case is to create and fan the flames of dispute, have reduced nearly every human interaction to a matter for the Law. Sure, some late-20th century practitioners began to pave the way for something called "Alternate Dispute Reso-lution," purportedly aimed at reducing the potential costs of litigation while making an effort at finding some compromise through mediation. But the atmosphere of battle is still in the air, and well-heeled litigators stand at the ready to engineer offensive strategies that only result in at least two disgruntled, discontented, unsatisfied and financially ruined parties.

In the criminal courts, those accused of crimes against the State, whose losses may well be greater than monetary, find their best defense is usually the costliest. Overworked Sixth-

Amendment court-appointed attorneys often provide little of value other than the dreaded plea bargain to those unfortunates without the financial means to hire the more expensive pros. And, as it is, the often corrupt, always iffy jury system is only now being exploited for its failures: Dozens of inmates in prisons across America are reluctantly setting lifers free after exonerating DNA evidence has cleared them of crimes juries of their peers were once certain they had committed. Creative members of the criminal bar are sparing no expense or energy as they work to circumvent the Law and the Constitution. Providing "zealous representation" to the wealthiest clients for a century, lawyers have given us a Constitution without teeth, one that nearly flies in the face of the intentions of the very men who framed it.

But, just like the economic meltdown we've all felt in this first decade of the 21st Century, perhaps no single group or entity is entirely responsible for the Frankenstein's monster we call The Law. Perhaps the greed of the people, battered by decades of injustice, coupled with a general moral failure within American society has led to a conscious reigning in of our personal benevolent reach—to the point of really only "looking out for number one." After all, given the near-constant barrage of lawyers advertising their services for an ever-growing basket of offenses, both real and imagined, who can blame the person who got rear-ended in a collision from "milking" it for all it's worth?

What person of modest means can resist the sales pitch of a well-dressed lawyer who insists that thirty years of cigarette smoking of your own volition is not your fault, but the fault of those mean-spirited and sneaky tobacco companies who lured you, tempted you, and filled their products with highly addictive substances? (*Especially when he drops the bit about the seven-figure award "you" will likely receive*).

I mean, your child is born with Cerebral Palsy and some lawyer like Jonathon Edwards comes along and insists that the defect is the fault of your obstetrician who failed to perform a timely Caesarian section which led to intra-natal hypoxia,[36] which led to the defect. You're hurting, your world is probably caving in, and you embrace the lawyer's assessment. The resulting award will help defray the costs of specialized care for you child (minus the legal fees and costs) as he grows and matures.

Later on, maybe years later, when you find out that only 1 per cent of all CP cases are the result of intra-natal hypoxia,[37] and your obstetrician, the one who'd already delivered 30,000 successful babies before, has had to go out of the baby-birthing business because of the half-million dollar malpractice insurance premium, will you reflect on what happened? Will you question your lawyer or yourself? Will you give it a second thought? Will you give the money back?

When you can't stop drinking or doing illegal drugs and your arrest record and your jail time keep increasing, will you blame society? Will you say that there are too many laws? Will you ever, *ever* take responsibility for your own actions?

When Hurricane Katrina devastated the Gulf region, persons in the media weren't so concerned about how to get people out as much as trying to determine "who's to blame." When the officials tell you to evacuate and you don't, and then you're injured or killed, whose fault is that? By the way, if after that storm you *chose* to move back into the teeth of the next cat, *you* are to blame. With the hundreds of thousands of places to live in this great country, if you choose to live in a city that resides

36 Oxygen starvation to the baby during the birthing process.
37. "Intrapartum Hypoxic-Ischemic Cerebral Injury and Subsequent Cerebral Palsy: Medicolegal Issues" by James Pearlman, Pediatrics, June 1977.

below the water line, don't ask me for help when the next flood comes along.

I spoke one time with a U.S. Coast Guardsman who was once assigned to their station in Key West, Florida. He told me stories of brief encounters with strangers who indicated to him that $20,000 could be his if only his little cutter happened *not* to be in a certain cove on a certain night. He never told me if he bit; but he indicated that he'd surely thought about it. Who could resist? Is that greed? Is that simply opportunity? Is it the fault of the drug-trafficker?

The Law has followed Newtonian physics down and down until you cannot even own a home of your own in a residential area without the ever-present and watchful eyes of your homeowner's association. In Florida, where I live, the plentiful numbers of retirees with nothing better to do with their time than to watch and complain about everything from the size of your dog to the color of the paint on your lanais to your American Flag are nothing more than an extension of the already suffocating Law. They, too, are tired of being victimized by the law, but see no other remedy than to re-inflict that same assault on their neighbors. They are unhappy with the pace of growth, or saddened by the encroaching specter of their own death, and they want to lash out, too. Too often, in an effort to demonstrate that while they are old they still have worth, they use the law to build themselves into their tiny fortresses, never to dispense upon the rest of us their gift of wisdom. They feel, like so many of the rest of us, that somebody, some*thing* is out to get them.

That thing is the Law.

Lawyers—the ones we're talking about in this book anyway—have traded much of what is valuable and beautiful in life for money, or what they feel it can buy: Something to fill the void inside of them. But it cannot fulfill, and it cannot sustain and it cannot satisfy. *You* need to understand and embrace this fact as well, because unless they can convince you of the same lie they are living, they have nothing. So far, of course, they've been quite convincing.

As I've said throughout this book, the Law is not a simple thing. To try to concentrate it in any one book would be a fool-hardy and frustrating exercise in futility. What I've tried to do is to confirm what you already know about the law, and to instill in you the belief that it doesn't have to be that way. No one person can change the world; but one person can change his or her corner of it. One person can have a positive effect upon those in his or her circle of influence, especially within the family. The Law is like a game of tennis, players serving and volleying and lobbing and smashing. But in the law, the object being struck is not a furry rubber ball filled with air, but We The People. And just like in a tennis match, if one player elects not to return the ball, the game is over. You can be that one player.

The Law will always be close, looming over us like the low ceiling in a camper trailer; that I can't help. We've little choice, if we decide to live in the United States, other than to do what it says or pay the consequences. Just remember, though, that whenever you find yourself in a predicament where you feel that you've been injured by the negligence of another, or been vic-timized by the intentional acts of another, ask yourself it you really want to hire a lawyer and add insult to injury. If your answer is "yes," then be prepared to be disappointed. Sure, you may win some money, and yeah, you might be made "whole." Or a criminal may be convicted and sent to prison for a time. But you will never get satisfaction, the kind of satisfaction that brings with it the soft pillow of peace, because the law does not and can not provide it.

And who's to blame for that?

Bradenton, Florida
March, 2009